T0212934

SpringerBriefs in Computer Science

Series Editors
Stan Zdonik
Shashi Shekhar
Jonathan Katz
Xindong Wu
Lakhmi C. Jain
David Padua
Xuemin (Sherman) Shen
Borko Furht
V.S. Subrahmanian
Martial Hebert
Katsushi Ikeuchi
Bruno Siciliano
Sushil Jajodia
Newton Lee

More information about this series at http://www.springer.com/series/10028

Zhuo Lu • Wenye Wang • Cliff Wang

Modeling and Evaluating Denial of Service Attacks for Wireless and Mobile Applications

Zhuo Lu
Department of Computer Science
University of Memphis
Memphis, TN, USA

Wenye Wang
Department of Electrical
   and Computer Engineering
North Carolina State University
Raleigh, NC, USA

Cliff Wang
Computing and Information Science Division
Army Research Office
Triangle Park, NC, USA

ISSN 2191-5768   ISSN 2191-5776 (electronic)
SpringerBriefs in Computer Science
ISBN 978-3-319-23287-4   ISBN 978-3-319-23288-1   (eBook)
DOI 10.1007/978-3-319-23288-1

Library of Congress Control Number: 2015952649

Springer Cham Heidelberg New York Dordrecht London

© The Author(s) 2015
This work is subject to copyright. All rights are reserved by the Publisher, whether the whole or part of the material is concerned, specifically the rights of translation, reprinting, reuse of illustrations, recitation, broadcasting, reproduction on microfilms or in any other physical way, and transmission or information storage and retrieval, electronic adaptation, computer software, or by similar or dissimilar methodology now known or hereafter developed.
The use of general descriptive names, registered names, trademarks, service marks, etc. in this publication does not imply, even in the absence of a specific statement, that such names are exempt from the relevant protective laws and regulations and therefore free for general use.
The publisher, the authors and the editors are safe to assume that the advice and information in this book are believed to be true and accurate at the date of publication. Neither the publisher nor the authors or the editors give a warranty, express or implied, with respect to the material contained herein or for any errors or omissions that may have been made.

Printed on acid-free paper

Springer International Publishing AG Switzerland is part of Springer Science+Business Media (www.springer.com)

Preface

The proliferation of wireless networks has brought significant change to people's daily life, such as WiFi and cellular networks. It further introduces new applications and services, including smart grid systems and emerging mobile services. However, due to the shared nature of wireless channels, these emerging applications are vulnerable to denial-of-service attacks, which come with various intents, from selfish sharing of channel resources to disrupting the communication among other users. A direct consequence of such attacks is performance degradation or even denial-of-service in the network. Moreover, they can lead to potentially devastating system failures, such as in the smart grid where physical control is all based on successful message delivery in the network. As a result, it is critical to understand the impact of denial-of-service attacks in emerging wireless applications.

This book compiles and summarizes our research results on studying DoS attacks in emerging wireless and mobile systems. Our objective is to understand the impact of DoS attacks, discover security vulnerabilities, and discuss and design corresponding countermeasures. We also notice that different applications have exhibited distinct features and objectives. For example, data-service networks (e.g., WiFi and cellular networks) aim at providing high upload/download throughput for clients, while time-critical networks (e.g., wireless networks for the smart grid) are designed to successfully deliver control messages within their deadlines for electronic devices. This in fact indicates that it is impractical to use a unified framework to measure the performance of all emerging wireless applications under DoS attacks. Therefore, our study is application-specific. In particular, our methodology is to first clearly identify DoS attacks associated with particular applications that can significantly affect network availability, then adequately define metrics to quantify their impacts, and finally discover or suggest solutions to mitigate such impacts on the network performance.

Our study starts from WiFi networks, since they are currently widely deployed across the world. As WiFi standards evolve, multi-modal WiFi networks emerge as a new type of WiFi networks that offer network connection to heterogeneous nodes equipped with various WiFi standards, such as 802.11a/b/g and 802.11e. To support such multi-modality, critical parameters in wireless adapters have become configurable to users. In other words, it becomes feasible to modify WiFi physical or MAC layer parameters, which in turn leads to a severe security issue. Specifically, numbers of existing wireless networks, such as WiFi or ZigBee, are based on the carrier-sensing multiple access with collision avoidance (CSMA/CA) mechanism, in which a distributed random backoff algorithm is used to coordinate all wireless nodes to fairly share the wireless channel. However, with configurable network adapters, a node can deliberately reduce its backoff time to gain unfair access to the channel at the cost of performance degradation or even denial-of-service of other legitimate nodes, which is called backoff misbehavior. A variety of backoff misbehavior models have been proposed so far to achieve unfair access to wireless resources. However, none of the existing research provides the answer to a fundamental question: What is a node's quantitative gain if it chooses to misbehave? This is very important for security designers to understand and defend against backoff misbehavior in WiFi networks or even all CSMA/CA-based wireless networks. Therefore, we are interested in offering a thorough study on how to categorize existing classes of backoff misbehavior in terms of their benefits and pointing out which type of misbehavior is the most harmful in CAMA/CA networks.

Quantifying the gain of backoff misbehavior can be regarded as a problem of modeling DoS attacks in the context of conventional data-access networks. Recently, emerging information systems and the advance of wireless technologies have extended the goal of wireless networking from providing conventional data access to a much broader scope. Time-critical wireless networks for cyber-physical systems, in particular the smart grid, are one of the most important new applications. Differing from conventional data-access networks, where throughput is one of the most important performance metrics, time-critical wireless networks for the smart grid aim at offering reliable and timely message delivery between physical devices. Thus, a large amount of communication traffic is time-critical (e.g., messages in power substations have latency constraints ranging from 3 to 500 ms). As a result, it is vital to guarantee network availability in terms of message delay performance instead of data throughput performance in time-critical wireless networks. However, on the other hand, the shared nature of wireless channels inevitably surrenders information delivery over such networks to jamming attacks, which may severely degrade the performance and reliability of these applications. Although there have been significant advances towards jamming characterization and countermeasures for conventional networks, little attention has been focused on jamming attacks targeting time-critical wireless networks in the context of the smart grid. Motivated by such emerging wireless applications and the severe threats from jamming attacks, we are interested in finding an appropriate performance metric to model the impact of jamming attacks against time-critical traffic, and try to accurately detect attacks that can severely affect the performance of time-critical applications.

Besides the goal of jamming modeling and detection, we also aim at providing countermeasures to defend against jamming attacks in time-critical applications for the smart grid. Existing jamming-resistant communication schemes are based on the spread spectrum techniques, which focus mainly on how a message can be delivered from the source to the destination under jamming attacks; that is, existing schemes focus on achieving *feasible* communication under jamming attacks. However, due to the time-critical nature of wireless smart grid applications, we require not only *feasible* communication, but also *timely* communication. Consequently, we are motivated to investigate solutions to minimize the message delay in time-critical wireless networks under jamming attacks.

At last, in addition to the emerging time-critical applications, the proliferation of smart handheld devices, ubiquitous wireless connectivity, and high-volume data centers introduce new smart phone services in mobile networks, such as mobile cloud services. Such mobile services also face significant security challenges due to mobile malware, which is malicious software targeting mobile applications. Statistics have shown that mobile malware has exploded in recent years. For example, from 2010 to 2011, mobile malware samples had exceeded 1300 with a more than 100 % increase overall and a 400 % increase in Android platforms. Moreover, a mobile botnet, which is a collection of compromised smart phones that can perform coordinated attacks, no longer occurs in theory. For example, *Ikee.B* in 2009 was found to include command and control logic to render a number of infected iPhones under the control. In 2012, Symantec found a large botnet *Android.Bmaster* in China that had infected an estimate of hundreds of thousands of Android phones. As a result, mobile botnets have already become one of the most serious security threats to today's mobile networks and applications. Despite such impendent threats in practice, little attention has been focused on analyzing how emerging data services are resilience to mobile malware epidemics. Therefore, this open question motivates us to model the resilience conditions of mobile cloud services against malware attacks.

In summary, our application-driven study of the impact of DoS attacks on emerging wireless and mobile applications greatly expands our knowledge on security issues and vulnerabilities in such applications, and meanwhile provides instrumental guidelines for the efficient, robust, and secure design of wireless networks for these applications.

Memphis, TN, USA   Zhuo Lu
Raleigh, NC, USA   Wenye Wang
Triangle Park, NC, USA   Cliff Wang
June 2015

Contents

Acronyms

CA	Collision Avoidance
CCDF	Complementary Cumulative Distribution Function
CSMA	Carrier-Sensing Multiple Access
DCF	Distributed Coordination Function
DIFS	DCF Inter-Frame Space
DoS	Denial-of-Service
DSSS	Direct-Sequence Spread Spectrum
FHSS	Frequency-Hopping Spread Spectrum
GOOSE	Generic Object Oriented Substation Event
IED	Intelligent Electronic Device
JADE	Jamming Attack Detection based on Estimation
LLR	Likelihood Ratio
MAC	Medium Access Control
MU	Merging Unit
NIST	National Institute of Standards and Technology
OFDM	Orthogonal Frequency-Division Multiplexing
P&C	Protection and Control
PN	Pseudo Noise
SMS	Short Message Service
SST	Solid-State Transformer
TACT	Transmitting Adaptive Camouflage Traffic
USRP	Universal Software Radio Peripheral

Chapter 1
Modeling and Evaluation of Backoff Misbehaving Nodes in CSMA/CA Networks

1.1 Motivation and Related Work

The carrier-sense multiple-access with collision avoidance (CSMA/CA) protocol, which is widely used in wireless networks such as IEEE 802.11 and IEEE 802.15, relies on a distributed backoff mechanism for efficient use of the shared channel. However, backoff misbehavior [12], which manipulates the backoff time at the medium access control (MAC) layer, is one of the easiest ways to obtain network resources at the cost of performance degradation [12] or even denial-of-service of legitimate nodes [20]. Hence, many works have been done to provide countermeasures to backoff misbehavior [3, 5, 8, 11, 12, 17, 18] based on a variety of misbehavior models. However, the behavior of a misbehaving node could be unpredictable in a wireless network. A misbehaving node can perform any type of misbehavior as long as it achieves sufficient benefits, which poses a challenging problem to the design of countermeasures. A recent work [15] indicates that it is not practical to design an omnipotent method to counter-attack all possible misbehaviors and further points out that countermeasures should focus on the misbehaving nodes with significant gains and at the same time neglect the misbehaving nodes with only marginal gains to save resources such as energy and bandwidth. Therefore, quantifying the performance gain of backoff misbehavior becomes a prerequisite to the design of countermeasures to backoff misbehavior.

To this end, a gain factor is proposed in [15] to indicate the impact of misbehavior. However, the gain factor is limited since it is assumed that there exists only one misbehaving node in the network and the backoff process of legitimate nodes is simplified to uniform backoff, which is inconsistent with the widely-used binary exponential backoff in CSMA/CA networks. Thus, a fundamental question remains unsolved: *how to quantify the gain of backoff misbehavior in CSMA/CA-based wireless networks?*

© The Author(s) 2015
Z. Lu et al., *Modeling and Evaluating Denial of Service Attacks for Wireless and Mobile Applications*, SpringerBriefs in Computer Science,
DOI 10.1007/978-3-319-23288-1_1

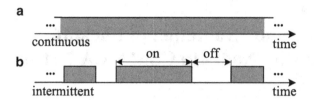

Fig. 1.1 Comparison between continuous backoff misbehavior and intermittent backoff misbehavior. (**a**) continuous misbehavior (**b**) intermittent misbehavior

In this chapter, we address the problem of quantifying the gain of backoff misbehavior. Our methodology is to study the gain that a misbehaving node can obtain via two general classes of backoff misbehavior. The first class is called *continuous misbehavior*, which performs misbehavior persistently and does not stop until it is disabled by countermeasures, as shown in Fig. 1.1a. Specially, we consider two extensively-adopted models of continuous misbehavior [3, 11, 12, 18]: (1) *double-window* backoff misbehavior, which conforms to the exponential backoff that is used by legitimate nodes, but has a smaller average backoff time than legitimate nodes. For example, the work in [18] defined the misbehavior model as *double-window* misbehavior and proposed a sequential hypothesis testing algorithm to detect the misbehavior; (2) *fixed-window* backoff misbehavior, which chooses the random backoff time uniformly in a given range. For example, the work in [3] considered *fixed-window* misbehavior as the easiest model for misbehaving nodes and designed an incentive-based protocol to discourage *fixed-window* misbehaving nodes and to motivate all nodes to achieve a Nash equilibrium.

The second class is called *intermittent misbehavior*, which in contrast to continuous misbehavior, performs misbehavior in *on* periods and returns to be legitimate in *off* periods, as shown in Fig. 1.1b. The goal of intermittent misbehavior is to obtain benefits over legitimate nodes and at the same time to evade misbehavior detection. Although existing literature mainly dealt with continuous misbehavior and focused little attention on intermittent misbehavior, the work in [17] has indicated that an intermittent misbehaving node may evade the detection of misbehavior detectors if the *on* period in which it performs misbehavior is smaller than the monitoring period of misbehavior detectors. However, the gain of intermittent misbehavior, especially the impact of intermittent misbehavior on a wireless network remains unknown yet.

We consider the two classes of backoff misbehavior in slotted CSMA/CA-based wireless networks, in which the time is measured by the number of idle slots.[1] In order to quantify the gain of backoff misbehavior, we introduce a new performance metric, namely *order gain* $G(t)$, as a function of waiting time t that denotes the

---

[1] The length of an idle slot varies upon different standards. For example, the durations of an idle slot is 20 μs in IEEE 802.11b for direct sequence spread spectrum (DSSS), and is 9 μs in IEEE 802.11g for orthogonal frequency-division multiplexing (OFDM) with 20 MHz channel spacing.

number of idle slots during a node contends for the channel. Then, we use the metric of order gain to analyze the benefits of the two classes of backoff misbehavior and further evaluate their impacts via simulations and experiments. Our contributions are threefold.

1. A new metric, order gain, is defined to measure the performance benefits of misbehaving nodes over legitimate nodes, which is helpful in evaluating the gain and impact of a misbehaving node in a CSMA/CA-based wireless network. Based on our analytical results, we quantify the performance gains of both *double-window* backoff misbehavior and *fixed-window* backoff misbehavior as well as the gain of intermittent backoff misbehavior.
2. We validate the impact of backoff misbehavior via simulations and experiments. We find that the number of users is a critical factor to the evaluation of countermeasures to backoff misbehaviors. Our results show that both *double-window* and *fixed-window* backoff misbehaviors can achieve significant gains when the number of users is small. Compared with *fixed-window* backoff misbehavior, *double-window* backoff misbehavior shows only marginal gains in a network with a large number of users. We also show that an intermittent misbehaving node can not achieve substantial gains when it only has a short *on* period.
3. We further show that backoff misbehaviors in IEEE 802.11 networks can be categorized into two classes: *finite-gain* misbehavior and *scalable-gain* misbehavior, in terms of the throughput gain ratio that is the ratio of the throughput of a misbehaving node to that of a legitimate node. A finite-gain misbehaving node always has upper-bounded throughput gain ratio; while a scalable-gain misbehaving node has throughput gain ratio proportional to the number of legitimate nodes in a network, which indicates that scalable-gain misbehaving nodes are much more harmful than finite-gain misbehaving nodes in large-scale networks.

The rest of this chapter is organized as follows. In Sect. 1.2, we introduce preliminaries and formulate the problem of quantifying the gain of backoff misbehavior. In Sect. 1.3, we present our main results of the order gains for misbehaving nodes via analytical modeling and simulations. In Sect. 1.4, we show the throughput gains of misbehaving nodes in IEEE 802.11 networks and further categorize backoff misbehavior in terms of the throughput gain. In Sect. 1.5, we present experimental results to show the impact of misbehaving nodes on a practical WiFi network. Finally, we conclude in Sect. 1.6.

1.2 Preliminaries and Problem Statement

In this section, we first introduce the models of backoff misbehavior, then define the order gain of backoff misbehaviors for later analysis.

1.2.1   CSMA/CA Backoff and Misbehaviors

In wireless networks, CSMA/CA features a distributed control algorithm for resolving packets collisions due to contending a shared channel by uncoordinated users. A widely-used collision resolution algorithm is *binary exponential backoff*, which has been adopted in many standards, such as Ethernet and 802.11 distributed coordination function (DCF). In binary exponential backoff, a node which has packets ready to transmit keeps sensing the channel until the channel is idle and then generates a random backoff time uniformly from $[0, w - 1]$, where w is called the *contention window*. At first w is set to be w_0, which is called the *minimum contention window*,[2] and is doubled after each collision. According to this procedure, we formally define legitimate CSMA/CA backoff as follows.

Definition 1.1 (Legitimate Binary Exponential Backoff).   The legitimate CSMA /CA backoff scheme $\mathscr{B}$ is defined as the backoff mechanism in which the random backoff time $T(i)$ is chosen uniformly from $[0, 2^i w_0 - 1]$ after the ith collision of a packet, where w_0 is the minimum contention window.

Remark 1.1.   Note that in practice, there are upper limits for the contention window as well as the number of retransmissions (e.g., 1024 and 7 in IEEE 802.11, respectively). In this chapter, we assume in our theoretical model that there are no upper limits on both the number of retransmissions and the contention window to facilitate our subsequent analysis. In other words, we adopt an asymptotic approach to analyze the gain of backoff misbehavior in CSMA/CA networks. We will investigate the effects of the two limits via simulations and experiments in Sect. 1.5.3.

Legitimate CSMA/CA backoff attempts to coordinate all nodes to efficiently share the same channel by assigning a node a longer backoff time with a higher probability after each collision, which in turn reduces the chance of the node to access the channel. Therefore, if one node intends to acquire the channel with a higher chance regardless of the others, the easiest solution is to reduce its backoff time, which is referred to as *backoff misbehavior* [12]. Note that CSMA/CA suffers several other fairness problems. For example, the near-far effect due to physical diversity in wireless LANs [6] results in a node with a better channel condition having a higher chance to access the channel. In this chapter, we assume that the unfairness in a wireless network is caused only by backoff misbehavior. It is also worth noting that the backoff behavior of several practical network cards has been shown to have some degree of violation of standard specifications [2], but we assume that all legitimate nodes use the same backoff scheme in Definition 1.1. The objective of a backoff misbehaving node is to gain unfair access to the channel by manipulating its backoff time at the cost of performance deterioration of legitimate

---

[2]The minimum contention window is the initial value of the contention window. For example, the minimum contention window is 32 in IEEE 802.11b for DSSS.

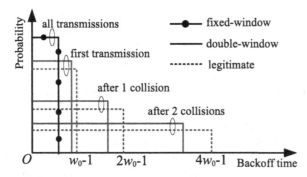

Fig. 1.2 Comparison between legitimate backoff, *double-window* misbehaving backoff and *fixed-window* misbehaving backoff

nodes. Therefore, backoff misbehaviors have been studied extensively because of their easy operation and potential catastrophic impact on network performance.

In the following, we describe two widely-studied backoff misbehavior schemes in the literature: *double-window* backoff misbehavior and *fixed-window* backoff misbehavior. In *double-window* backoff misbehavior, as shown in the solid line of Fig. 1.2, a misbehaving node conforms to the binary exponential backoff, but uses a smaller minimum contention window than w_0. For example, *double-window* backoff misbehavior was considered in both [12] and [7] as the backoff misbehavior model and was shown to achieve substantial performance gains over legitimate nodes. Thus, we can see from Fig. 1.2 that compared to the legitimate backoff scheme, which is shown as dashed lines, a *double-window* misbehaving node always has a higher chance to access the channel after each collision. For *fixed-window* backoff misbehavior which is shown by dotted solid lines in Fig. 1.2, a misbehaving node never increases its contention window and always chooses backoff time uniformly from a fixed interval. Thus, it has a much higher chance to access the channel than legitimate nodes. Formally, we have the definitions for these two types of backoff misbehavior as follows:

Definition 1.2 (*Double-Window* Backoff Misbehavior). A *double-window* misbehaving node uses backoff scheme $\mathcal{B}_D$ in which the random backoff time $T_D(i)$ is chosen uniformly from $[0, 2^i w_D - 1]$ after the ith collision, where $w_D < w_0$.

Definition 1.3 (*Fixed-Window* Backoff Misbehavior). A *fixed-window* misbehaving node uses backoff scheme $\mathcal{B}_F$ in which the random backoff time $T_F(i)$ is chosen uniformly from $[0, w_F - 1]$ after the ith collision, where $w_F < w_0$.

Remark 1.2. Both *double-window* and *fixed-window* backoff misbehaviors share a common feature; that is, once they start to misbehave, they never stop unless they are disabled by countermeasures. Thus, we refer them also *continuous misbehavior* because such misbehaving nodes constantly manipulate their backoff time to obtain unfair access to the channel.

It is worthy of note that a misbehaving node may not perform a particular backoff scheme all the time. For example, it is implied in [17] that a misbehaving node may evade misbehavior detection if it frequently changes backoff schemes. This type of misbehavior can be characterized as *intermittent misbehavior*, which performs misbehavior sporadically. Therefore, in this study, we further consider such type of misbehavior in order to thoroughly understand the impact of misbehaving nodes in CSMA/CA-based wireless networks.

In order to evade misbehavior detection, an intermittently misbehaving node only performs misbehavior in the *on* state and returns to legitimate behavior in the *off* state. Therefore, it has two backoff schemes: the misbehaving (on-state) and legitimate (off-state) backoff schemes, either of which can be used to transmit a packet. Such an intermittently misbehaving node can choose its status by following various criteria. For example, it can switch (on/off) status memorylessly or based on history. In this work, we assume that an intermittently misbehaving node chooses its next status based on the current status; i.e., we define intermittent misbehavior with a Markov chain with two states as follows.

Definition 1.4 (Intermittent Backoff Misbehavior). Given the legitimate backoff scheme $\mathscr{B}$ and a misbehaving backoff scheme $\mathscr{B}_m$, the backoff scheme of inter-mittent backoff misbehaving nodes is defined as a Markov process $\{\mathscr{B}_I(n); n = 0, 1, 2, \ldots\}$, where n denotes the nth packet to be transmitted, $\mathscr{B}_I(n) \in \{\mathscr{B}, \mathscr{B}_m\}$. Transition probabilities from $\mathscr{B}$ to $\mathscr{B}_m$ and from $\mathscr{B}_m$ to $\mathscr{B}$ are denoted by α and β, respectively. The on-state ratio $\theta \in (0, 1)$ is defined as the steady-state probability of $\mathscr{B}_I(n) = \mathscr{B}_m$, i.e., $\theta \triangleq \alpha/(\alpha + \beta)$.

Remark 1.3. As shown in Fig. 1.3, an intermittently misbehaving node can fre-quently switch its state between *on* and *off* with backoff schemes $\mathscr{B}_m$ or $\mathscr{B}$, respectively. Our definition of intermittent misbehavior is generic since the mis-behaving scheme $\mathscr{B}_m$ in *on* state is not constrained to be a specific misbehaving backoff scheme.

So far, we have defined the models for both continuous and intermittently misbehaving nodes. In the next section, we will introduce a new metric to quantity the benefits of backoff misbehaving nodes.

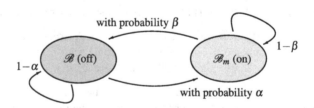

Fig. 1.3 The *on* and *off* states in intermittent backoff misbehavior

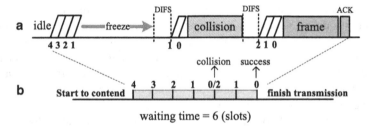

Fig. 1.4 A packet transmission process in IEEE 802.11. (**a**) transmission process (**b**) slotted waiting time

1.2.2 Definition of Order Gain

In general, the benefits of misbehaving nodes are improving their occupancy of resources and achieving better performance. The network performance, on the other hand, can be evaluated by a number of metrics, such as the most commonly-used throughput and delay [1, 22]. However, the two performance metrics depend highly on protocol specifications. For example, Fig. 1.4a illustrates a simple transmission process in IEEE 802.11 DCF. During the transmission, we can see that the packet delay includes the idle slot time, freezing time, DCF Interframe Space (DIFS) interval, and the packet transmission time. If we consider the same transmission process under a different MAC protocol, such as ZigBee or even different 802.11 models, the packet delay will change because of distinct protocol specifications. However, we do not want our analysis to be limited to a particular MAC protocol as CSMA/CA is extensively adopted in wireless networks. Therefore, we attempt to extract the essential backoff part of CSMA/CA from a MAC protocol by deleting all protocol-related signals, as shown in Fig. 1.4b.

We name the resultant process as the backbone process since it is protocol-independent and consists of a number of slots induced only by a random backoff mechanism. In the backbone process, we define the waiting time of a node as follows.

Definition 1.5 (Waiting Time). The waiting time of a node, W, is the total number of counted slots induced by counter decrements between the instant that the node starts to contend for the channel and the instant that the node successfully captures the channel; that is, $W \triangleq \sum_{i=0}^{N} T(i)$, where N is the number of collisions before the node makes a successful transmission and $T(i)$ is the random backoff time (counted by slots) after the ith collision.

From Fig. 1.4b, we see that the waiting time during the transmission is six slots, which is not dependent on protocol signals and the time duration of a slot, but is determined only by a backoff mechanism. Thus, it can be considered as a generic performance metric for CSMA/CA. Note that the waiting time has the limitation of measuring the real-time delay performance when dealing with a particular CSMA/CA protocol such as 802.11, since it neglects protocol specifications such as counting-down freezing and DIFS signals. However, it is still clear that a node's throughput (or delay) is in fact a consequence of its waiting time. For example, if a node's waiting time is zero (meaning that it never waits to transmit), its packet delay should be very small and its throughput is almost equal to the channel bandwidth. Thus, waiting time can immediately represent the performance of a node with a backoff mechanism: the shorter the waiting time, the better the performance (i.e., higher throughput and shorter delay).

On the other hand, although waiting time can characterize the performance of a node, our objective is *not* to evaluate the performance of a single node but to understand benefits of backoff misbehaving schemes, that is the *gain* of misbehaving nodes over legitimate nodes. To this end, we introduce a *new* performance metric by considering the following constraints:

1. This metric should not be subject to a particular protocol because of the wide deployment of CSMA/CA networks, such as IEEE 802.11 and IEEE 802.15. Therefore, the definitions of control messages, such as DIFS, ACK should not affect the interpretation of the *gain*. Hence, we choose the protocol-independent waiting time W as a basis for our performance metric. We use the tail distribution function $\mathbb{P}(W > t)$ to represent the waiting time since it is a random variable.
2. If nodes A and B have the same backoff scheme, the gain of node A over node B should be zero.
3. If the gain of node A over node B is G_1 and the gain of node B over node C is G_2, then the gain of node A over node C follows the additive rule, that is, $G_1 + G_2$. This property is very important because it enables us to quantitatively compare the impacts of two misbehaving nodes by directly comparing their metrics.

Keeping these requirements in mind, we introduce a new metric, namely *order gain* of waiting time[3] as follows.

Definition 1.6 (Order Gain of Waiting Time). Let W_A and W_B be the waiting times of nodes A and B, respectively. The order gain of node A over node B is defined as

$$G(t) \triangleq \log_t \frac{\mathbb{P}(W_B > t)}{\mathbb{P}(W_A > t)}, \ (t > 0) \tag{1.1}$$

where $\mathbb{P}(W_A > t)$ and $\mathbb{P}(W_B > t)$ are the tail distribution functions (or complementary cumulative distribution functions, CCDFs) of W_A and W_B, respectively.

Remark 1.4. As shown in (1.1), the order gain is defined as the logarithm of the ratio between two tail distribution functions to the base of t. Note that any base in fact satisfies the three requirements. Here, we choose the base of t since the operator of $\log_t(\cdot)$ can yield the slope values of widely-used power-law distributions in log-log

---

[3]The order gain of waiting time will be simplified as *order gain* thereafter; unless specified otherwise.

scales for large t, which in turn means that for such distributions, the order gain has an approximate geometric interpretation, i.e., the slope difference between the tail distribution functions of misbehaving and legitimate nodes on log-log scales.

1.3   Order Gains of Misbehaving Backoff Schemes

In this section, we present our analytical results on quantifying the gain of backoff misbehavior. In particular, we first study the two continuous misbehaviors: *double-window* misbehavior and *fixed-window* misbehavior. Then, we move on to the intermittent misbehavior.

1.3.1   Double-Window Backoff Misbehavior

A *double-window* misbehaving node, which is defined in Definition 1.2, adopts binary exponential backoff but uses a smaller minimum contention window than the legitimate nodes. In order to find the order gain of *double-window* misbehaving nodes, it is essential to obtain the tail distribution functions of waiting time for *double-window* misbehaving nodes and the legitimate nodes. We first derive the tail distribution function of the waiting time of legitimate nodes in the following lemma.

Lemma 1.1. *Let p be the collision probability[4] of a legitimate node. Based on Definition 1.1, the tail distribution function of waiting time of a legitimate node $\mathbb{P}(W > t)$ is lower and upper bounded by*

$$\frac{p^2}{4}\left(\frac{t}{w_0}+1\right)^{\log_2 p} \le \mathbb{P}(W > t) \le \frac{1}{p}\left(\frac{t}{w_0}+1\right)^{\log_2 p} \tag{1.2}$$

for all t sufficiently large.

Proof. From Definition 1.5, the waiting time of a legitimate node can be written as $W = \sum_{i=0}^{N} T(i)$, where N is the number of collisions before the node makes a successful transmission. Given collision probability p, $\mathbb{P}(N = j) = (1 - p)p^j$. $T(i) \in [0, 2^i w_0 - 1]$ is the random backoff time after the ith collision. Let $\{W > t\}$ be the event that waiting time W is larger than t, which means that there is no successful transmission of the node in $[0, t]$. Since $T(i)$ is upper bounded by $2^i w_0 - 1$, a necessary condition for holding $\{W > t\}$ is that there are at least ρ collisions, where $\rho = \min \mathscr{X}$ and $\mathscr{X} = \{x : \sum_{i=0}^{x}(2^i w_0 - 1) \ge t\}$. Since $\rho \in \mathscr{X}$, we have $\sum_{i=0}^{\rho}(2^i w_0 - 1) \ge t$ and have a lower bound of ρ

---

[4]Throughout this chapter, we define the collision probability of a node as the probability that there is at least one other node transmitting when the node sends a packet. We also assume that it always holds that a collision probability is in $(0,1)$ for our analytical analysis.

$$\rho \geq \log_2(t/w_0 + 1) - 1. \tag{1.3}$$

Meanwhile, ρ is the minimum in $\mathscr{X}$, which means $\rho - 1 \notin \mathscr{X}$ and $\sum_{i=0}^{\rho-1} (2^i w_0 - 1) < t$. Then, we have an upper bound of ρ

$$\rho \leq \log_2(t/w_0 + 1) + 1. \tag{1.4}$$

Thus, the tail distribution function $\mathbb{P}(W > t)$ can be represented as

$$\mathbb{P}(W > t) = \sum_{j=\rho}^{\infty} \mathbb{P}(N = j)\mathbb{P}\left(\sum_{i=0}^{N} T(i) > t | N = j\right) \leq \sum_{j=\rho}^{\infty} \mathbb{P}(N = j) = p^\rho. \tag{1.5}$$

It follows from (1.3) and (1.5) that

$$\mathbb{P}(W > t) \leq \frac{1}{p}\left(\frac{t}{w_0} + 1\right)^{\log_2 p}, \tag{1.6}$$

which completes the proof of the upper bound.

Now we derive the lower bound of $\mathbb{P}(W > t)$. We first separate $\{W > t\}$ into two disjoint events: $\{W > t\} = \{t < W \leq \sum_{i=0}^{\rho}(2^i w_0 - 1)\} \cup \{W > \sum_{i=0}^{\rho}(2^i w_0 - 1)\}$; then,

$$\mathbb{P}(W > t) \geq \mathbb{P}\left(W > \sum_{i=0}^{\rho}(2^i w_0 - 1)\right) = \sum_{k=\rho+1}^{\infty} \mathbb{P}(N = k)\,\mathbb{P}(E_k), \tag{1.7}$$

where event $E_k = \{\sum_{i=0}^{N} T(i) > \sum_{i=0}^{\rho}(2^i w_0 - 1) | N = k\}$ for $k = \rho+1, \rho+2, \cdots$. We further have

$$E_{\rho+1} = \left\{\sum_{i=0}^{\rho+1} T(i) > (2^{\rho+1} - 1)w_0 - (\rho+1)\right\}$$

$$\supset \{T(\rho+1) + T(\rho) > (2^{\rho+1} - 1)w_0 - (\rho+1)\}, \tag{1.8}$$

where $T(\rho + 1)$ and $T(\rho)$ are uniformly distributed on $[0, 2^{\rho+1}w_0 - 1]$ and $[0, 2^\rho w_0 - 1]$, respectively. Thus,

$$\mathbb{P}(E_{\rho+1}) \geq \mathbb{P}\left(T(\rho+1) + T(\rho) > (2^{\rho+1} - 1)w_0 - (\rho+1)\right)$$

$$= \frac{(2^\rho w_0 - 1)/2 + w_0 + \rho}{2^{\rho+1}w_0} \geq \frac{1}{4}. \tag{1.9}$$

Similarly, we have

$$\mathbb{P}(E_k) \geq \frac{1}{4}, \text{ for } k = \rho+2, \rho+3, \cdots. \tag{1.10}$$

By substituting (1.4) and (1.10) into (1.7), we obtain the lower bound

$$\mathbb{P}(W > t) \geq \frac{p^2}{4} \left(\frac{t}{w_0} + 1 \right)^{\log_2 p}. \tag{1.11}$$

$\square$

With Lemma 1.1, we state our main result on the order gain of *double-window* misbehavior as follows.

Theorem 1.1. *The order gain of a* double-window *backoff misbehaving node over legitimate nodes is*

$$G_D(t) = \log_2 \left(\frac{p}{p_D} \right) + \Theta \left(\frac{1}{\ln t} \right), {}^{5}$$

where p and p_D are the collision probabilities of the legitimate and misbehaving nodes, respectively.

Proof. The order gain of the *double-window* misbehaving node over legitimate nodes is defined as

$$G_D(t) = \log_t \frac{\mathbb{P}(W > t)}{\mathbb{P}(W_D > t)}, \tag{1.12}$$

where $\mathbb{P}(W > t)$ and $\mathbb{P}(W_D > t)$ are the tail distribution functions of waiting time for legitimate nodes and the *double-window* misbehaving node, respectively. From Lemma 1.1, the tail distribution function of waiting time of legitimate nodes can be represented as

$$\mathbb{P}(W > t) = \Theta \left((t/w_0 + 1)^{\log_2 p} \right). \tag{1.13}$$

Since a *double-window* misbehaving node also adopts binary exponential backoff, we can have

$$\mathbb{P}(W_D > t) = \Theta \left((t/w_D + 1)^{\log_2 p_D} \right), \tag{1.14}$$

---

[5] We say function $f(x)$ is of the same order as function $g(x)$ and write $f(x) = \Theta(g(x))$ if and only if there exist two positive real numbers c_1 and c_2 and a real number x_0 such that $c_1|g(x)| \leq |f(x)| \leq c_2|g(x)|$ for all $x > x_0$.

where w_D and p_D are the minimum contention window and collision probability of *double-window* misbehaving node, respectively. By substituting (1.13) and (1.14) into (1.12), we obtain $G_D(t) = \log_2(p/p_D) + \Theta(1/\ln t)$.   □

Remark 1.5. According to Theorem 1.1, the order gain of *double-window* misbehaving nodes, $G_D(t)$, converges to $\log_2(p/p_D)$ as $t \to \infty$, showing that the order gain can be determined by collision probabilities of legitimate and misbehaving nodes. In this work, we do not discuss how to calculate these collision probabilities, but it has been shown in [16] that the ratio $p/p_D \to 1$ as the number of nodes goes to infinity. Therefore, the order gain of a *double-window* misbehaving node will approach zero when the number of nodes increases to infinity.

To attest our models and analytical results, we use the ns2 simulator to evaluate the performance of *double-window* backoff misbehavior by considering an 802.11 network in the presence of one *double-window* backoff misbehaving node and five legitimate nodes. In addition, we use the following setups for our simulations: we generate saturated traffic at all misbehaving and legitimate nodes. There is no upper limit for the contention window or the number of retransmissions for any node. The minimum contention window of legitimate nodes is $w_0 = 16$.

We first show in Fig. 1.5 the empirical order gains of the misbehaving node compared with theoretical results $\log(p/p_D)$ in Theorem 1.1 for different minimum contention windows $w_D = 6, 8, 10, 12$. Note that the collision probabilities p and p_D are measured during simulations. As [16] has shown that $\log(p/p_D)$ is a decreasing function of both w_D and the number of nodes, Fig. 1.5 illustrates that the order gain is indeed inversely proportional to w_D: the larger the minimum contention

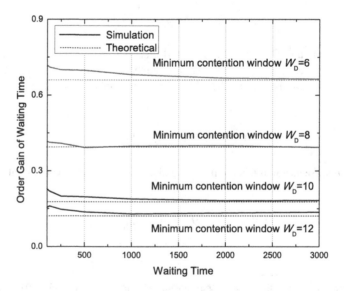

Fig. 1.5 Order gains of a *double-window* backoff misbehaving node with minimum contention window $w_D = 6, 8, 10$, and 12 in an 802.11 network in the presence of five legitimate nodes

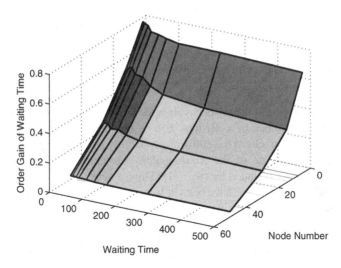

Fig. 1.6 Order gains of a *double-window* backoff misbehaving node with minimum contention window $w_D = 6$ in an 802.11 network with different numbers of legitimate nodes

window w_D, the smaller the order gain. Figure 1.5 also shows that with increasing waiting time t, the order gain converges monotonically to the constant $\log(p/p_D)$ as predicated in Theorem 1.1, even through the convergence rate is low. Then, in Fig. 1.6, we fix the minimum contention window of the misbehaving node to be $w_D = 6$ and show the order gain of the *double-window* misbehaving node for different numbers of legitimate nodes in the network. We also observe that the order gain of the misbehaving node decreases as the number of legitimate nodes increases. For example, the order gain of the misbehaving node converges to 0.02 when the number of legitimate nodes is equal to 50, which validates our statement that the order gain of *double-window* misbehaving nodes approaches zero with increasing the number of nodes in Remark 1.5.

1.3.2 Fixed-Window Backoff Misbehavior

Another widely-adopted continuous misbehaving scheme is *fixed-window* backoff misbehavior. A *fixed-window* backoff misbehaving node, as defined in Definition 1.3, never increases its contention window in order to achieve frequent access to the channel. Next, we first derive the tail distribution function of its waiting time, followed by the analysis of its order gain, $G_F(t)$.

Lemma 1.2. *For a* fixed-window *misbehaving node, the tail distribution function of its waiting time* $\mathbb{P}(W_F > t)$ *is lower and upper bounded by*

$$\frac{1}{w_F} e^{\frac{t}{w_F-1}\ln(p_F/w_F)} \leq \mathbb{P}(W_F > t) \leq e^{\left(\frac{t}{w_F-1}-1\right)\ln p_F},$$

where w_F and p_F are the minimum contention window and collision probability of the misbehaving node, respectively.

Proof. The waiting time of the misbehaving node can be written as $W_F = \sum_{i=0}^{N_F} T_F(i)$, where N_F is the number of collisions before the misbehaving node makes a successful transmission. Given the collision probability p_F, $\mathbb{P}(N_F = j) = (1-p_F)p_F^j$. $T_F(i)$ is the backoff time of the *fixed-window* misbehaving node after the ith collision, and is upper bounded by $(w_F - 1)$. Thus, a necessary condition for event $\{W_F > t\}$ holding is that there have been at least $\rho_F = \lfloor t/(w_F - 1)\rfloor$ collisions. The tail distribution function of waiting time of the misbehaving node can be written as

$$\mathbb{P}(W_F > t) = \sum_{j=\rho_F}^{\infty} \mathbb{P}(N_F = j)\mathbb{P}\left(\sum_{i=0}^{N_F} T_F(i) > t | N_F = j\right)$$

$$\leq \sum_{j=\rho}^{\infty} \mathbb{P}(N_F = j) = p_F^{\rho_F} \leq e^{\left(\frac{t}{w_F-1}-1\right)\ln p_F}. \tag{1.15}$$

On the other hand, if $T_F(0), T_F(1), \ldots, T_F(\rho_F)$ are all equal to $w_F - 1$, we have

$$\sum_{i=0}^{N_F} T_F(i) \geq \sum_{i=0}^{\rho_F} T_F(i) = (\rho_F + 1)(w_F - 1) \geq t \tag{1.16}$$

since $N_F \geq \rho_F = \lfloor t/(w_F - 1)\rfloor$. Then

$$\mathbb{P}\left(\sum_{i=0}^{N_F} T_F(i) > t | N_F = j\right) \geq \mathbb{P}(T_F(0) = \ldots = T_F(\rho_F) = w_F - 1) = (1/w_F)^{\rho_F+1}. \tag{1.17}$$

Consequently, we have

$$\mathbb{P}(W_F > t) = \mathbb{P}\left(\sum_{i=0}^{N_F} T_F(i) > t\right) \geq \sum_{j=\rho_F}^{\infty} \mathbb{P}(N_F = j)\left(\frac{1}{w_F}\right)^{\rho_F+1}$$

$$= \frac{1}{w_F}\left(\frac{p_F}{w_F}\right)^{\rho_F} \geq \frac{1}{w_F} e^{\frac{t}{w_F-1}\ln(p_F/w_F)}, \tag{1.18}$$

which finishes the proof.   □

With Lemma 1.2, we are ready to present the main result on the order gain of *fixed-window* backoff misbehavior.

Theorem 1.2. *The order gain of a* fixed-window *backoff misbehaving node over legitimate nodes is* $G_F(t) = \Theta\left(\frac{t}{\ln t}\right)$.

The proof is similar to Theorem 1.1. The order gain of a *fixed-window* backoff misbehaving node is represented by

$$G_F(t) = \log_t \frac{\mathbb{P}(W > t)}{\mathbb{P}(W_F > t)}. \tag{1.19}$$

Using the bounds of $\mathbb{P}(W > t)$ in Lemma 1.1 and the bounds of $\mathbb{P}(W_F > t)$ in Lemma 1.2 can finish the proof.

Remark 1.6. Theorem 1.2 tells that the order gain of *fixed-window* backoff misbehavior is an increasing function to infinity as $t \to \infty$ regardless of the number of nodes in the network. This implies that a misbehaving node can always obtain substantial benefits from *fixed-window* backoff misbehavior. Thus, any countermeasure to backoff misbehavior should consider *fixed-window* backoff misbehavior as its primary target.

Next we present simulation results regarding the order gain of *fixed-window* backoff misbehavior. We use the same network setups in Fig. 1.5. But the misbehaving node will perform *fixed-window* backoff misbehavior instead of *double-window* backoff misbehavior. The fixed contention window of the misbehaving node is set to be $w_F = 6, 8, 10, 12$. Figure 1.7 shows the order gain of the misbehaving node for

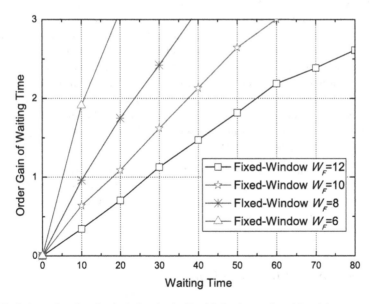

Fig. 1.7 Order gain of a *fixed-window* backoff misbehaving node with minimum contention window $w_F = 6, 8, 10,$ and 12 in an 802.11 network in the presence of five legitimate nodes

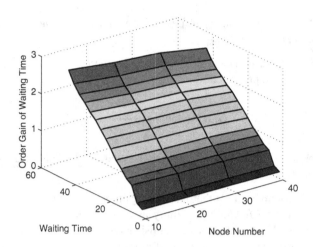

Fig. 1.8 Order gains of a fixed-window backoff misbehaving node with fixed contention window $w_F = 8$ in an 802.11 network with different numbers of legitimate nodes

different w_F. It is observed from Fig. 1.7 that the order gain of the *fixed-window* backoff misbehaving node keeps increasing sub-linearly as t increases. This is because the order gain of fixed-window misbehavior is at the order of a sub-linear function $t/\log(t)$ as shown in Theorem 1.2. Note also that the increasing rate of the order gain of *fixed-window* misbehavior depends on w_F. Thus, theoretically, *fixed-window* misbehavior with a small w_F can have very large values of order gain even when the waiting time t is small.

We also consider the impact of the number of legitimate nodes on the order gain of the misbehaving node, as shown in Fig. 1.8. It is noted from Fig. 1.8 that compared with the *double-window* backoff misbehaving node in Fig. 1.6, the number of legitimate nodes does not have a significant effect on the order gain of the *fixed-window* backoff misbehaving node. As shown in Fig. 1.8, the order gain always increases as the waiting time increases, regardless of the number of legitimate nodes, implying that in general, *fixed-window* backoff misbehavior can obtain larger gain than *double-window* backoff misbehavior.

Remark 1.7. Compared with *double-window* backoff misbehavior, *fixed-window* backoff misbehavior can be much more harmful to a wireless network. Therefore, *fixed-window* backoff misbehavior should always be the primary target of counter-measures to backoff misbehavior.

1.3.3   Intermittent Backoff Misbehavior

We have studied the order gains of two widely-used backoff schemes for continuous misbehavior. However, a misbehaving scheme is not always guaranteed to be continuous, especially when there exists a counter-strategy in the network which aims to detect and disable misbehaviors. It has been shown in [17] that a node performing misbehavior intermittently may evade such misbehavior detection. Thus, it is important to understand the benefits of such an intermittent misbehaving in a wireless network. The backoff scheme of an intermittently misbehaving node is defined as a Markov process with *on* and *off* states in Definition 1.4. With this definition, we have

Theorem 1.3. *For an intermittently misbehaving node with on-state ratio θ, assume that when it changes its states, all nodes can immediately re-enter steady states. Then, its order gain satisfies $G_I(t) = \log_2 \frac{p_{on}}{p_{off}} + \Theta\left(\frac{1}{\ln t}\right)$, where p_{on} and p_{off} are steady-state collision probabilities of legitimate nodes in on and off states, respectively.*

Proof. The order gain of an intermittently misbehaving node is defined as

$$G_I(t) = \log_t(\mathbb{P}(W > t)/\mathbb{P}(W_I > t)), \tag{1.20}$$

where $\mathbb{P}(W > t)$ and $\mathbb{P}(W_I > t)$ are the tail distribution functions of the waiting time for legitimate and intermittently misbehaving nodes, respectively. The probabilities of the intermittently misbehaving node being in *on* and *off* states are $\mathbb{P}(\text{on}) = \theta$ and $\mathbb{P}(\text{off}) = 1 - \theta$, respectively. Note that though legitimate nodes do not change their backoff scheme, they are affected by the change of status of the intermittently misbehaving node, therefore also have *on* and *off* states. Then, we have

$$\mathbb{P}(W > t) = \theta \mathbb{P}(W > t | \text{on}) + (1 - \theta)\mathbb{P}(W > t | \text{off}) \tag{1.21}$$

$$\text{and} \quad \mathbb{P}(W_I > t) = \theta \mathbb{P}(W_I > t | \text{on}) + (1 - \theta)\mathbb{P}(W_I > t | \text{off}), \tag{1.22}$$

respectively. Substituting (1.22) and (1.21) into (1.20) yields

$$G_I(t) = \log_t\left(\frac{\theta + (1 - \theta)t^{-G(t)}}{\theta t^{-G_{on}(t)} + (1 - \theta)t^{-G(t)}}\right), \tag{1.23}$$

where $G_{on}(t) = \log_t \frac{\mathbb{P}(W > t | \text{on})}{\mathbb{P}(W_I > t | \text{on})}$ is called *all-on order gain*, and $G(t) = \log_t \frac{\mathbb{P}(W > t | \text{on})}{\mathbb{P}(W > t | \text{off})}$ is called *on-off legitimate order gain*, which is due to the difference between the collision probabilities p_{on} and p_{off} of legitimate nodes in *on* and *off* states, respectively. Since $G(t)$ can be regarded as the order gain of a double-window misbehaving node over a legitimate node with collision probabilities p_{on} and p_{off}, respectively. We reuse Theorem 1.1 and obtain that

$$G(t) = \log_2 \frac{p_{on}}{p_{off}} + \Theta\left(\frac{1}{\ln t}\right). \tag{1.24}$$

Since the misbehaving node can always obtain gains from its backoff misbehavior when it is *on*, it holds that $\mathbb{P}(W_I > t|\text{on}) \leq \mathbb{P}(W > t|\text{off})$. Thus, $G_{on}(t) \geq G(t)$ and $\theta t^{-G_{on}(t)} \leq \theta t^{-G(t)}$. Then, from (1.23), we have found the lower bound

$$G_I(t) \geq \log_t \left(\frac{\theta + (1-\theta)t^{-G(t)}}{\theta t^{-G(t)} + (1-\theta)t^{-G(t)}} \right) \geq \log_t \left(\frac{\theta}{t^{-G(t)}} \right) = G(t) + \frac{\ln\theta}{\ln t}. \quad (1.25)$$

On the other hand, it follows from (1.23) that

$$G_I(t) \leq \log_t \left(\frac{\theta + (1-\theta)t^{-G(t)}}{(1-\theta)t^{-G(t)}} \right). \quad (1.26)$$

Because $G(t)$ converges to $\log_2(p_{on}/p_{off}) > 0$, there exists a constant t_0 such that $t^{-G(t)} \leq 1$ for all $t > t_0$, and then (1.26) can be upper bounded by

$$G_I(t) \leq \log_t \left(\frac{\theta + (1-\theta)}{(1-\theta)t^{-G(t)}} \right) = G(t) - \frac{\ln(1-\theta)}{\ln t} \quad (1.27)$$

for all $t > t_0$. Combining (1.24), (1.25), and (1.27) yields

$$G_I(t) = \log_2 \frac{p_{on}}{p_{off}} + \Theta\left(\frac{1}{\ln t} \right). \quad (1.28)$$

$\square$

Theorem 1.3 shows that, perhaps surprisingly, the order gain of an intermittently misbehaving node $G_I(t)$ always converges to a constant that does not depend on θ. In the following, we use simulations to investigate the effect of θ on the order gain of intermittent misbehavior.

We consider an 802.11 network consisting of five legitimate nodes and one intermittently misbehaving node in simulations. The intermittently misbehaving node chooses a random backoff time uniformly from $[0,7]$ when it is in on-state. Figure 1.9 demonstrates the order gains of the intermittently misbehaving node for different on-state ratios θ. We see from Fig. 1.9 that the order gain of the misbehaving node always exhibits an initial increasing phase, and after reaching a maximum, it starts to converge decreasingly. This reveals an interesting phenomena that there exists a *phase transition phenomenon* in the order gain of intermittent misbehavior. The phase transition phenomenon is more evident when θ becomes large. We denote by t^* the phase transition point, which is the value of waiting time corresponding to the maximum of the order gain. During simulations, we find that t^* increases as θ increases, but the increment is not significant. For example, in Fig. 1.9, t^* increases from 18 to 33 as θ goes from 50 to 99%.

Figure 1.9 also shows that the order gain of an intermittently misbehaving node is not significant when θ is small. For example, when $\theta = 50\%$, the order gain is always smaller than 0.35 and the phase transition phenomenon is not evident.

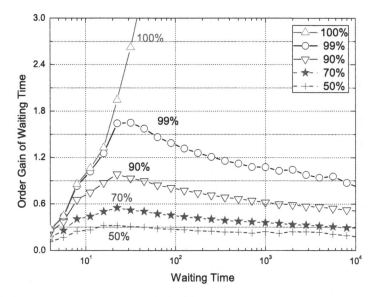

Fig. 1.9 Order gain of an intermittently misbehaving node in a network with five legitimate nodes

When $\theta = 70\%$, the order gain is also upper bounded by 0.6. Consequently, our simulation results indicate that if an intermittently misbehaving node attempts to evade misbehavior detection by choosing a small θ, it cannot achieve large values of order gain. An extreme case is that when $\theta = 0$, there is no performance gain of intermittent nodes which cannot degrade network performance because it always follows the legitimate backoff scheme.

On the other hand, if an intermittently misbehaving node chooses a large θ to achieve substantial gains, it may not be able to evade misbehavior detection in that it appears similarly as a continuous misbehaving node. For example, we can see in Fig. 1.9 that when the intermittently misbehaving node has $\theta = 99\%$, its order gain is almost the same as $\theta = 100\%$ for small waiting time t. In this case, the intermittently misbehaving node has a higher risk to be detected.

We have provided ns2 simulation results for both continuous and intermittent misbehaviors. To further verify our analytical modeling and derivation, we consider a more heterogenous network with five legitimate nodes, one *fixed-window* misbehaving node, one *double-window* misbehaving node, and an intermittently misbehaving node with $\theta = 90\%$ that performs *fixed-window* misbehavior in its on-state. Figure 1.10 shows the simulation results on the order gains for different misbehaving nodes in this scenario. As we can see from Fig. 1.10, the order gain of the *fixed-window* misbehaving node always increases as the waiting time increases; the order gain of the *double-window* misbehaving node is approximately a constant; and the order gain of the intermittently misbehaving node has a phase transition phenomenon and eventually converges as the waiting time increases.

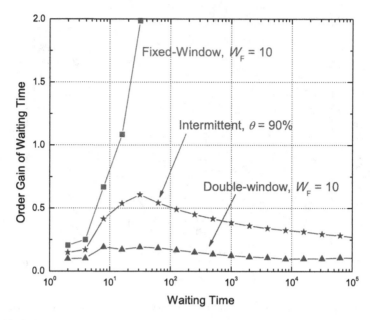

Fig. 1.10 Order gains of various misbehaving nodes in an 802.11 network with five legitimate nodes

Figure 1.10 validates that our analytical results on assessing the order gains of misbehaving nodes are general and depend on neither the number of legitimate and misbehaving nodes nor the heterogeneity of a CSMA/CA-based wireless network.

1.4   From Order Gain to Throughput Gain

We have so far investigated the performance gains of continuous and intermittently misbehaving nodes via the metric of order gain, which is a general metric to quantify backoff misbehavior in CSMA/CA-based wireless networks. For IEEE 802.11 DCF that becomes ubiquitous nowadays, the order gain-based analysis of previous misbehavior models is also applicable since the metric of order gain is based on the essential waiting time that is measured by the number of slots and does not depend on any specific protocol. However, the MAC layer throughput of a node is one of the most widely-used metrics in 802.11 DCF (e.g. [1, 4, 9, 14]). Moreover, the throughput, unlike the order gain, can directly reflect how much data a node has transmitted over a time period. Thus, it is of great interest to investigate how much throughput gain a misbehaving node can obtain from legitimate nodes in an 802.11 network.

In the following, we consider the basic access model in IEEE 802.11 DCF as our primary protocol model. We assume that the idle slot length and packet length are fixed to be σ and L (measured by μs), respectively. We also assume that all nodes are in saturated state. It has been shown in the literature (e.g., [1, 4, 9, 14]) that it is difficult to derive a closed-form throughput formula for a node working under IEEE 802.11 DCF. Therefore, our goal in this section is not to derive the exact throughput gain for a certain type of backoff misbehaving nodes, but to show the relation between the metric of order gain and throughput gain of a misbehaving node in an IEEE 802.11 network. Formally, we define a misbehaving node's throughput gain over legitimate nodes as follows.

Definition 1.7. Let the access delay of a node be the real-time interval (measured by μs) from the instant that the node begins to contend for the channel to the instant that the node finishes a successful transmission. Then, the saturated throughputs of a legitimate node and a misbehaving node are defined as

$$S = L/\mathbb{E}(D), \quad \text{and} \tag{1.29}$$

$$S_m = L/\mathbb{E}(D_m), \tag{1.30}$$

where D and D_m are the access delays of the legitimate node and the misbehaving node, respectively. The throughput gain ratio for the misbehaving node is defined as the ratio between the saturated throughputs of the misbehaving node and the legitimate node; i.e.,

$$R_m = S_m/S = \mathbb{E}(D)/\mathbb{E}(D_m). \tag{1.31}$$

Remark 1.8. From (1.31), we can see the throughput gain ratio is essentially the ratio between the mean access delays of the legitimate node and the misbehaving node. Therefore, in the following, we obtain the desirable throughput gain ratio by computing the ratio between mean access delays for legitimate and misbehaving nodes.

With Definition 1.7, we state our main results about the throughput gain of backoff misbehaving nodes as follows.

Theorem 1.4 (Throughput Gain Ratio). *In an IEEE 802.11 network with n legitimate nodes and a backoff misbehaving node, assume that all nodes use the same physical layer parameters (e.g., modulation and error-correction coding). If the order gain of the misbehaving node $G_m(t)$ satisfies $\lim_{n,t\to\infty} G_m(t) = 0$, the throughput gain ratio of the misbehaving node is always upper-bounded, i.e.,*

$$\lim_{n\to\infty} R_m(n) < \infty. \tag{1.32}$$

If $G_m(t)$ satisfies $\lim_{n,t\to\infty} G_m(t) > 0$, the throughput gain ratio of the misbehaving node goes to infinity as $n \to \infty$, i.e.,

$$\lim_{n\to\infty} R_m(n) = \infty. \tag{1.33}$$

Proof. The proof consists of two parts.

Part I. $(\lim_{n,t\to\infty} G_m(t) = 0 \Rightarrow \lim_{n\to\infty} R_m(n) < \infty)$

The access delay for 802.11 DCF has been well modeled and studied in the literature. Following the model of access delay for 802.11 DCF in [19], the mean access delays of a legitimate node and a misbehaving node can be represented as

$$\mathbb{E}(D) = ((1-p)\sigma + pL)\mathbb{E}(W) + \frac{L}{1-p}, \quad \text{and} \tag{1.34}$$

$$\mathbb{E}(D_m) = ((1-p_m)\sigma + p_m L)\mathbb{E}(W_m) + \frac{L}{1-p_m}, \tag{1.35}$$

respectively, where p and p_m are the collision probabilities of the legitimate node and misbehaving node, respectively. As shown in [16], the collision probability p is an increasing function of n and converges to 0.5. Then, from Lemma 1.1, the mean waiting time of a legitimate node satisfies that $\lim_{n\to\infty} \mathbb{E}(W) = \infty$.

Since the order gain of the misbehaving node converges to 0; i.e.,

$$\lim_{n,t\to\infty} G_m(t) = \lim_{n,t\to\infty} \log_t \frac{P(W > t)}{P(W_m > t)} = 0, \tag{1.36}$$

From Lemma 1.1 and (1.36), we have

$$\lim_{n,t\to\infty} \left(\log_t \frac{p^2}{4} \left(\frac{t}{w_0} + 1 \right)^{\log_2 p} - \log_t P(W_m > t) \right) = 0, \quad \text{and}$$

$$\lim_{n,t\to\infty} \log_t P(W_m > t) = \lim_{n\to\infty} \log_2 p = -1, \tag{1.37}$$

which indicates that W_m also asymptotically follows the power-law distribution with the same parameter of $\lim_{n\to\infty} -\log_2 p = 1$ as W. Thus, $\lim_{n\to\infty} \mathbb{E}(W)/\mathbb{E}(W_m)$ is always upper bounded although $\mathbb{E}(W)$ and $\mathbb{E}(W_m)$ go to infinity, respectively. Therefore, the throughput gain ratio can be represented as

$$\lim_{n\to\infty} R_m(n) = \lim_{n\to\infty} \frac{\mathbb{E}(D)}{\mathbb{E}(D_m)} = \lim_{n\to\infty} \frac{((1-p)\sigma + pL)\mathbb{E}(W) + \frac{L}{1-p}}{((1-p_m)\sigma + p_m L)\mathbb{E}(W_m) + \frac{L}{1-p_m}}$$

$$= \lim_{n\to\infty} \frac{(1-p)\sigma + pL + \frac{L}{(1-p)\mathbb{E}(W)}}{((1-p_m)\sigma + p_m L)\frac{\mathbb{E}(W_m)}{\mathbb{E}(W)} + \frac{L}{(1-p)\mathbb{E}(W)}}. \tag{1.38}$$

Since $\lim_{n\to\infty}(\mathbb{E}(W)/\mathbb{E}(W_m))$ is upper bounded and $\lim_{n\to\infty}((1-p_m)\sigma + p_m L) \neq 0$, we finally obtain from (1.38) that

$$\lim_{n\to\infty} R_m(n) < \infty. \tag{1.39}$$

Part II. $(\lim_{n,t\to\infty} G_m(t) > 0 \Rightarrow \lim_{n\to\infty} R_m(n) = \infty)$ First, the order gain of the misbehaving node satisfies

$$\lim_{n,t\to\infty} G_m(t) = \lim_{n,t\to\infty} \log_t \frac{\mathbb{P}(W > t)}{\mathbb{P}(W_m > t)} = \varepsilon > 0. \tag{1.40}$$

From Lemma 1.1 and (1.36), we have

$$\lim_{n,t\to\infty} \left(\log_t \frac{p^2}{4} \left(\frac{t}{w_0} + 1 \right)^{\log_2 p} - \log_t P(W_m > t) \right) \le \varepsilon, \quad \text{and}$$

$$\lim_{n,t\to\infty} \log_t P(W_m > t) \ge \lim_{n\to\infty} \log_2 p - \varepsilon = -(\varepsilon + 1), \tag{1.41}$$

which indicates that W_m asymptotically follows the power-law distribution with parameter $1 + \varepsilon > 1$ and $\mathbb{E}(W_m)$ is always well-defined, i.e., $\lim_{n\to\infty} \mathbb{E}(W_m) < \infty$. Therefore, from (1.38), the throughput gain ratio is $\lim_{n\to\infty} R_m(n) = \infty$. Combining the two parts completes the proof.   □

Remark 1.9.   Theorem 1.4 shows that any backoff misbehavior yields one of two consequences as the number of legitimate nodes increases: (1) the throughput gain ratio is bounded above, (2) the throughput gain ratio goes to infinity. Theorem 1.4 further indicates that all backoff misbehavior models can be in fact categorized into two types in terms of harmfulness. The first type of misbehavior always has upper-bounded throughput gain ratio, regardless the number of users in a network. Thus, we refer this type of misbehavior as *finite-gain backoff misbehavior*. The second type of misbehavior can be more harmful and its throughput gain ratio goes to infinity as the number of users increases. We refer it *scalable-gain backoff misbehavior*, which implies the gain of this type of misbehavior is scalable: the larger the network scale, the more the gain of the misbehaving node.

In previous sections, based on the basic backoff structure of misbehaving nodes, we generalized misbehavior models into continuous misbehavior and intermittent misbehavior. From Theorem 1.4, we can categorize backoff misbehavior models into finite-gain misbehavior and scalable-gain misbehavior in terms of the throughput gain ratio. Thus, existing misbehaviors can be formally separated into the two types in terms of their throughout gains, as shown in Table 1.1. The throughout gain obtained by misbehaving nodes, on the other hand, indicates that there exists throughput degradation of all legitimate nodes. The larger the gain of a misbehaving node, the larger the throughput degradation of legitimate nodes. We show in the following that when the number of nodes increases in a network, finite-gain misbehavior has only negligible impact on the network.

Table 1.1 Classifying backoff misbehaviors in terms of throughput gain

	Finite-gain	Scalable-gain
	Double-window misbehavior, intermittent misbehavior	Fixed-window misbehavior

Definition 1.8 (Throughput Degradation Ratio). Let S and S_m be the throughputs of a legitimate node and a backoff misbehaving node in a wireless network. Let S_l be the throughput of a legitimate node when all misbehaving nodes do not perform any misbehavior; i.e., S_l is the throughput that a legitimate node should have. Then, the throughput degradation ratio of a legitimate node due to backoff misbehavior is defined as

$$R_d = 1 - S/S_l. \tag{1.42}$$

Theorem 1.5 (Impact of Finite-Gain Backoff Misbehavior). *In an IEEE 802.11 network in the presence of n legitimate nodes and n_m backoff misbehaving nodes with the same physical-layer parameters. If the misbehaving nodes are all finite-gain misbehaving and n_m is fixed, then the throughput degradation ratio of a legitimate node, R_d satisfies that*

$$\lim_{n \to \infty} R_d = 0. \tag{1.43}$$

Proof. We assume that the channel bandwidth is normalized into 1 and is efficiently shared by legitimate nodes and misbehaving nodes, i.e.,

$$nS + n_m S_m = 1. \tag{1.44}$$

For the finite-gain misbehaving nodes, it always holds that

$$S_m/S \leq c, \tag{1.45}$$

where c is a sufficiently large constant. Thus, it follows from (1.44) and (1.45) that $1/n \geq S \geq 1/(cn_m + n)$. If all misbehaving nodes perform legitimately, we have $S_l = 1/(n + n_m)$. Therefore, we can obtain

$$\lim_{n \to \infty} \frac{1/n}{1/(n + n_m)} \geq \lim_{n \to \infty} \frac{S}{S_l} \geq \lim_{n \to \infty} \frac{1/(cn_m + n)}{1/(n + n_m)},$$

and $\lim_{n \to \infty} S/S_l = 1$.

Finally, the throughput degradation ratio of a legitimate node is

$$\lim_{n \to \infty} R_d = 1 - \lim_{n \to \infty} S/S_l = 1 - 1 = 0.$$

$\square$

Remark 1.10. In general, the deployment cost of a countermeasure increases as the number of nodes increases since the countermeasure needs to not only monitor states of all nodes, but also consistently perform computations based on their activities to detect any misbehavior (e.g. [21]). Existing work [15] has indicated that countermeasures to backoff misbehavior should be more concerned with misbehaving nodes that can significantly affect the network performance. Based on our analytical results, we suggest that *in large-scale networks, countermeasures to backoff misbehavior should focus primarily on scalable-gain misbehavior* since when the number of nodes is large, the effect of finite-gain misbehavior becomes marginal from a *damage perspective* as shown in Theorem 1.5.

1.5 Performance Evaluation and Discussions

In previous sections, we have investigated the performance gains of a variety of backoff misbehaviors in wireless networks. Based on analytical analysis and simulations, we used both the metric of order gain and the metric of throughput gain ratio to quantify how many benefits a backoff misbehaving node can obtain. To further evaluate the performance gain of misbehaving nodes and the impact of backoff misbehavior on a practical wireless network, we use off-the-shelf IEEE 802.11 products and the Madwifi driver [13] to set up an experimental WiFi network in the presence of a misbehaving node. Note that Madwifi is an advanced WiFi driver for Atheros chipsets. It provides application-layer interfaces for users to modify WiFi physical-layer parameters, such as the minimum contention window and the retry limit.

1.5.1 Experiment Setup

Network Deployment The experimental network consists of six laptops and two iPAQ pocket PCs with plug-in wireless cards. The laptops and pocket PCs are associated with a Cisco Access Point (Aironet 1200 series) working under IEEE 802.11b. There is no other access point working during our experiments. We place all devices inside a laboratory to ensure that they are under the same channel condition. The only difference between legitimate and misbehaving nodes is the backoff scheme. The other parameters, such as physical-layer rate and retry limit, are set up with the same values in all nodes. As it is difficult to find a completely interference-free environment, we perform all experiments at midnight to minimize the impact of interference on our experimental results.

Network Traffic The commonly-used network testing tool, *Iperf* [10], is used to generate traffic over the network. We use *Iperf* to generate UDP streams at the rate of 10 Mbps that can fill up the transmission queue at each device such that all devices are in saturated state.

Performance Metric It is not easy to accurately measure the waiting time at the MAC layer, since commercial 802.11 adapters do not expose their internal parameters to higher layers. Therefore, in our experiments, throughput of each node is measured for performance evaluation.

1.5.2   Experimental Results

Throughout our experiments, legitimate nodes always adopt the binary exponential backoff: the minimum and maximum contention windows are 32 and 65,536, respectively. The retry limit for both legitimate and misbehaving nodes is set to be 16. Here, we set large values for the maximum contention window and the retry limit to validate our asymptotic analysis.

We first study the performance gain of *double-window* and *fixed-window* misbehaving schemes. Figure 1.11 shows the throughput gain ratio of a *double-window* misbehaving node as a function of the minimum contention window of the misbehaving node and the number of legitimate nodes. We can see from Fig. 1.11 that the through gain ratio of the misbehaving node decreases as the minimum contention window increases and that the throughput gain ratio remains approximately the same when the number of legitimate nodes increases, which validates our analytical results in Sect. 1.4 showing that the throughput gain ratio

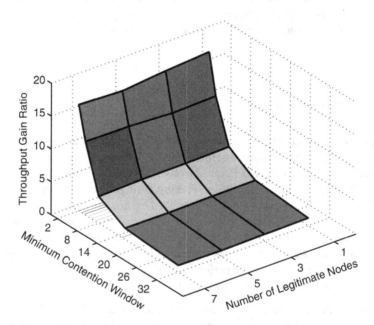

Fig. 1.11 Throughput ratio of a *double-window* backoff misbehaving node to a legitimate node for different backoff misbehaving schemes

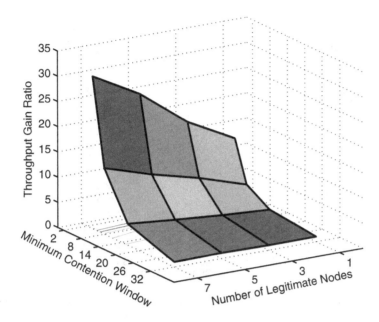

Fig. 1.12 Throughput ratio of a *fixed-window* backoff misbehaving node to a legitimate node

is always upper bounded. According to Theorem 1.5, we can expect that when the number of legitimate nodes increases in the network, *double-window* misbehavior only causes negligible performance degradation of legitimate nodes.

Figure 1.12 shows the throughput gain ratio of a *fixed-window* misbehaving node as a function of the minimum contention window of the misbehaving node and the number of legitimate nodes. From Fig. 1.12, we observe that the throughput gain ratio of the *fixed-window* misbehaving node is proportional to the number of legitimate nodes: the more the number of legitimate nodes, the larger the throughput gain ratio of the misbehaving node. For example, when the contention window of the *fixed-window* misbehaving node is 4, the throughput gain ratio increases from 12.9 to 30.2 as the number of legitimate nodes goes from 1 to 7. Figure 1.12 validates our results in Table 1.1, which shows that *fixed-window* backoff misbehavior belongs to scalable-gain misbehavior.

From Figs. 1.11 and 1.12, we see that if the number of legitimate nodes is small, *double-window* backoff misbehavior and *fixed-window* backoff misbehavior have similar throughput gain. If the number of legitimate nodes increases, *fixed-window* backoff misbehavior has much more gain than *double-window* backoff misbehavior. For example, when the misbehaving node has a minimum contention window of 8 and the number of legitimate nodes is 1, both *double-window* backoff misbehavior and *fixed-window* backoff misbehavior have approximate throughput gain ratio of 4.5. When the number of legitimate nodes becomes 7, the throughput gain ratio of *double-window* backoff misbehavior is still about 4.5 but that of *fixed-window* backoff misbehavior reaches 13. We can conclude that the number of users should

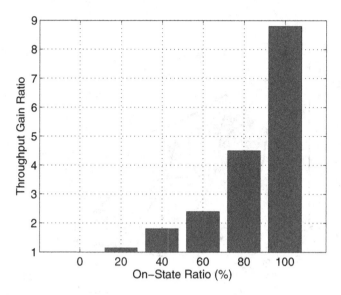

Fig. 1.13 Throughput ratio of the misbehaving node to a legitimate node for different on-state ratios θ

be considered as a critical factor to the evaluation of providing countermeasures to a network. When the number of users is small, countermeasures can focus on both *double-window* and *fixed-window* misbehaviors. When the number of users is large, countermeasures can focus only on *fixed-window* misbehavior since the gain of *double-window* misbehavior is always bounded and therefore it can only cause negligible performance degradation of legitimate nodes, as indicated in Theorem 1.5.

We then study the performance of intermittent misbehavior by considering a one-bad and five-good scenario. The intermittently misbehaving node chooses its random backoff time uniformly from $[0,7]$ in the *on* state and performs legitimate backoff in the *off* state. Figure 1.13 demonstrates the throughput ratio of the intermittently misbehaving node to a legitimate one, as a function of on-state ratio θ. We observe that the throughput ratio does not increase linearly with the increasing of θ, and the ratio is large only when θ is very large. The reason is that θ denotes the switching probability of misbehavior. For example, when $\theta = 50\%$, it switches between on and off states. From the time perspective, it in fact spends more time (large than 50%) on legitimate behavior since it has smaller access probability when behaving legitimately. Therefore, the overall throughput of the intermittently misbehaving node is less than 50% even when $\theta = 50\%$. Thus, a node has to choose a large θ to obtain significant benefits from intermittent misbehavior.

1.5.3 Effects of Upper Limits on Retransmissions and Contention Window

Our theoretical models are based on the assumption that there is no upper limit on either the number of retransmissions or the contention window. As there always exist such upper limits in practice, we discuss via both simulations and experiments the impact of these upper limits on our theoretical results.

We first use ns2 simulations to evaluate the effect of the upper limits. We set up an IEEE 802.11 network with one misbehaving node and five legitimate nodes. The minimum contention windows for legitimate and misbehaving nodes are 32 and 8, respectively. For all nodes, the upper limit of the contention window is 1024 (the same as that in IEEE 802.11); and the upper limit of the number of transmissions of a single packet (denoted by N_R) varies from 3 to 7. All nodes are saturated.

Figure 1.14 illustrates the order gain of the misbehaving node when it chooses double-window misbehavior. From Fig. 1.14, we can find that the finite value of N_R leads to a *finite region phenomenon* for the order gain: as waiting time t increases, the order gain dramatically increases to infinity. In other words, the order gain is finite only when t is sufficiently small. This is because the tail distribution of the waiting time for the misbehaving node $\mathbb{P}(W_D > t)$ will become zero when t is large enough. For example, when $N_R = 3$, the misbehaving node will attempt to transmit a packet 3 times before it drops the packet. Therefore the maximum possible waiting time is $8+16+32 = 56$. Then, it is impossible that the waiting time W_D is larger than

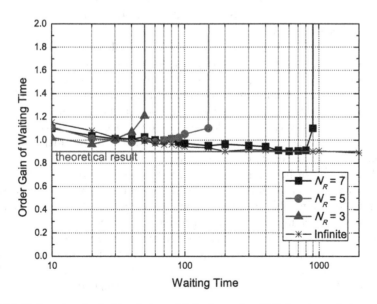

Fig. 1.14 Order gains of a double-window misbehaving node with finite retransmissions

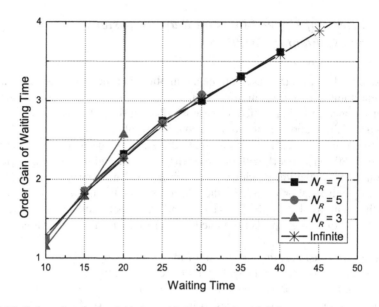

Fig. 1.15 Order gains of a fixed-window misbehaving node with finite retransmissions

56, leading to $\mathbb{P}(W_D > 56) = 0$. Accordingly, the order gain $G_D(t) = \log_t(P(W > t)/P(W_D > t))$ increases to infinity as t approaches 56.

Figure 1.15 shows the order gain of the misbehaving node when it chooses fixed-window misbehavior. We can also see the *finite region phenomenon* in Fig. 1.15: the order gain of the fixed-window misbehavior dramatically increases to infinity when the waiting time t is large enough.

Figures 1.14 and 1.15 indicate that we have to evaluate the order gain of a misbehaving node at its finite region (e.g., t is small) when considering a practical scenario; otherwise, the order gain will become infinity. We can see that the order gain with infinite retransmissions is still a good approximation of that with finite retransmissions, especially for fairly large N_R. For example, in Fig. 1.14, the order gain of $N_R = 7$ always has similar values to the order gain of $N_R = \infty$ when $t < 900$.

Next, we investigate how this *finite region phenomenon* of the order gain affects our theoretical results on throughput analysis. We consider an IEEE 802.11b network with one misbehaving node and a varying number of legitimate nodes. The setups are the same as those in Sect. 1.5.1, except that all nodes have the same upper limit for the number of transmissions for a single packet N_R. In addition, the maximum contention window for all nodes is set to be 1024. The minimum contention windows of legitimate and misbehaving nodes are 32 and 8, respectively.

Figure 1.16 illustrates the throughput gain ratio of the misbehaving node as a function of the number of legitimate nodes. It can be found in Fig. 1.16 that the smaller the retry limit N_R, the smaller the throughput gain ratio of the

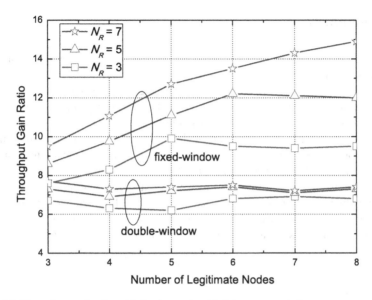

Fig. 1.16 Throughput gain of a misbehaving node with finite retransmissions

misbehaving node. This is because when a legitimate node has a smaller N_R, it will more frequently start a new transmission by resetting its contention window to the minimum, having more chance to access the channel. Figure 1.16 shows that the throughput gain ratio of double-window misbehavior is approximately the same regardless of the number of legitimate nodes; while that of fixed-window misbehavior increases proportionally to the number of legitimate nodes. However, the finite value of N_R imposes an upper bound on the throughput gain ratio of fixed-window misbehavior. For example, the upper bound is 9.9 and 12.1 when $N_R = 3$ and 5, respectively.

Figure 1.16 indicates that with upper limits of the contention window and the number of retransmissions, the finite-gain misbehavior (e.g., *double-window*) still has a finite throughput gain ratio; while scalable-gain misbehavior (e.g. *fixed-window*) has a throughput gain ratio that initially increases as the number of legitimate nodes increases, but also has an upper bound when the number of legitimate nodes is sufficiently large. We conclude from Fig. 1.16 that analytical results in Theorem 1.4 partially hold in practical scenarios and that such upper limits alleviate the damage caused by misbehaving nodes. However, scalable-gain misbehavior should still be a primary focus for countermeasures in that its throughput gain ratio remains scalable before approaching the upper bound that increases with the increasing of N_R.

1.6 Summary

In this chapter, we provided an in-depth study on the benefits of backoff misbehaving nodes by analytical modeling, simulations and experiments. We introduced a metric, *order gain*, to investigate two widely-used continuous misbehavior models: *double-window* and *fixed-window* backoff misbehaviors, and intermittent misbehavior that performs misbehavior intermittently to evade misbehavior detection. Besides our theoretical quantification of the gains of continuous and intermittent misbehaviors, we formally categorized backoff misbehavior into finite-gain misbehavior and scalable-gain misbehavior. We showed that *double-window* backoff misbehavior belongs to finite-gain misbehavior and has negligible impact on a network with a large number of users; *fixed-window* backoff behavior is much more harmful than others because it has scalable gain, which means its throughput gain ratio goes to infinity as the number of legitimate nodes increases to infinity.

References

1. Bianchi G (2000) Performance analysis of the IEEE 802.11 distributed coordination function. IEEE J Sel Areas Commun 18(3):535–547
2. Bianchi G, Stefano AD, Giaconia C, Scalia L, Terrazzino G, Tinnirello I (2007) Experimental assessment of the backoff behavior of commercial IEEE 802.11b network cards. In: Proceedings of IEEE INFOCOM'07, pp 1181–1189
3. Cagalj M, Ganeriwal S, Aad I, Hubaux JP (2005) On selfish behavior in CSMA/CA networks. In: Proceedings of IEEE INFOCOM'05, vol 4, pp 2513–2524
4. Cali F, Conti M, Gregori E (2000) Dynamic tuning of the IEEE 802.11 protocol to achieve a theoretical throughput limit. IEEE/ACM Trans Netw 8(6):785–799
5. Cardenas AA, Radosavac S, Baras JS (2007) Performance comparison of detection schemes for MAC layer misbehavior. In: Proceedings of IEEE INFOCOM'07, pp 1496–1504
6. Choi S, Park K, Kim CK (2005) On the performance characteristics of WLANs: revisited. In: Proceedings of ACM SIGMETRICS '05, pp 97–108
7. Guang L, Assi C, Benslimane A (2008) Enhancing IEEE 802.11 random backoff in selfish environments. IEEE Trans Veh Technol 57(3):1806–1822
8. Guang L, Assi C, Benslimane A (2008) MAC layer misbehavior in wireless networks: challenges and solutions. IEEE Wirel Commun 15(4):6–14
9. Hui J, Devetsikiotis M (2005) A unified model for the performance analysis of IEEE 802.11e EDCA. IEEE Trans Commun 53(9):1498–1510
10. Iperf (2013). http://sourceforge.net/projects/iperf/
11. Konorski J (2006) A game-theoretic study of CSMA/CA under a backoff attack. IEEE/ACM Trans Netw 14(6):1167–1178
12. Kyasanur P, Vaidya NH (2003) Detection and handling of MAC layer misbehavior in wireless networks. In: Proceedings of IEEE DSN'03, pp 173–182
13. Madwifi (2010). http://madwifi.org
14. Malone D, Duffy K, Leith D (2007) Modeling the 802.11 distributed coordination function in nonsaturated heterogeneous conditions. IEEE/ACM Trans Netw 15:159–172
15. Radosavac S, Baras JS, Koutsopoulos I (2008) An analytic framework for modeling and detecting access layer misbehavior in wireless networks. ACM Trans Inf Syst Secur 11(4):19:1–19:28

16. Ramaiyan V, Kumar A, Altman E (2005) Fixed point analysis of single cell IEEE 802.11e WLANs: uniqueness, multistability and throughput differentiation. In: Proceedings of ACM SIGMETRICS '05, pp 109–120

17. Raya M, Aad I, Hubaux J, Fawal AE (2006) DOMINO: detecting MAC layer greedy behavior in IEEE 802.11 hotspots. IEEE Trans Mob Comput 5(12):1691–1705

18. Rong Y, Lee SK, Choi HA (2005) Detecting stations cheating on backoff rules in 802.11 networks using sequential analysis. In: Proceedings of IEEE INFOCOM'06

19. Sakurai T, Vu HL (2007) MAC access delay of IEEE 802.11 DCF. IEEE Trans Wireless Commun 6(5):1702–1710

20. Szott S, Natkaniec M, Canonico R, Pach AR (2008) Impact of contention window cheating on single-hop IEEE 802.11e MANETs. In: Proceedings of IEEE WCNC'08, pp 1356–1361

21. Toledo AL, Wang X (2007) Robust detection of selfish misbehavior in wireless networks. IEEE J Sel Areas Commun 25(6):1124–1134

22. Ziouva E, Antonakopoulos T (2002) CSMA/CA performance under high traffic conditions: throughput and delay analysis. Comput Commun 25:313–321

Chapter 2
Modeling the Impact of Jamming Attacks on Time-Critical Traffic with Applications to Smart Grid

2.1 Motivation and Related Work

The advances of today's wireless technologies (e.g., 3G/4G and WiFi) has already brought significant change and benefit to people's life, such as ubiquitous wireless Internet access, mobile messaging and gaming. On the other hand, it also enables a new line of applications for emerging cyber-physical systems, in particular for the smart grid [19], where wireless networks have been proposed for efficient message delivery in electric power infrastructures to facilitate a variety of intelligent mechanisms as dynamic energy management, relay protection and demand response [2, 11, 18, 26].

Differing evidently from conventional communication networks, where throughput is one of the most important performance metrics to indicate how much data can be delivered during a time period, wireless networking for cyber-physical systems aims at offering reliable and timely message delivery between physical devices. In such systems, a large amount of communication traffic is time-critical (e.g., messages in power substations have latency constraints ranging from 3 to 500 ms [10]). The delivery of such messages is expected to be followed by a sequence of actions on physical infrastructures. Over-due message delivery may lead to instability of system operations, and even cascading failures. For instance, in the smart grid, a binary result of fault detection on a power feeder can trigger subsequent operations of circuit breakers [14]. If the message containing such a result is missed, or does not arrive on time, the actions on circuit breakers will be delayed, which can cause fault propagation along physical infrastructures and potential damages to power equipments.

As a result, it is critical to guarantee network availability in terms of message delay performance instead of data throughput performance in such time-critical applications, which is also considered as one of the most challenging issues in cyber-physical systems. However, on the other hand, the shared nature of wireless

© The Author(s) 2015
Z. Lu et al., *Modeling and Evaluating Denial of Service Attacks for Wireless and Mobile Applications*, SpringerBriefs in Computer Science, DOI 10.1007/978-3-319-23288-1_2

channels inevitably surrenders information delivery over wireless networks to jamming attacks [3, 21, 27], which may severely degrade the network performance and reliability by broadcasting radio interference over the shared wireless channel.

Although there have been significant advances towards jamming characterization [3, 21, 27] and countermeasures [4, 12, 13, 17, 20, 23–25] for conventional networks, little attention has been focused on jamming against message delivery in time-critical wireless applications. In particular, conventional performance metrics cannot be readily adapted to measure the jamming impact against time-critical messages. In conventional wireless networks, the impact of jamming attacks is evaluated at the packet level such as packet send/delivery ratio [27] and the number of jammed packets [12] (because existing data services are based on packet-switched networks), or at the network level such as saturated network throughput [3]. However, packet-level and network-level metrics do not directly reflect the latency constraints of message exchange in time-critical applications. For example, 100 % packet delivery ratio does not necessarily mean that all messages can be delivered on time to ensure reliable operations in a cyber-physical system.

In addition, lack of the knowledge on how jamming attacks affect such time-critical messaging leads to a gray area in the design of jamming detection; that is, it is not feasible to determine whether a jamming detection solution is effective or not, since detectors are not able to accurately identify jamming attacks with abilities to severely affect time-critical message delivery and further delay appropriate operations of physical devices. Therefore, towards emerging wireless applications in cyber-physical systems, an open and timely research question is *how to model, analyze, and detect jamming attacks against time-critical message delivery?*

In this chapter, we *study the problem of modeling and detecting jamming attacks in time-critical wireless applications.* Specifically, we consider two general classes of jamming attacks that are widely adopted in the literature: reactive jamming and non-reactive jamming [27]. The former refers to those attacks [13, 20, 23, 27] that stay quiet when the wireless channel is idle, but start transmitting radio signals to undermine ongoing communication as soon as they sense activity on the channel. The latter, however, is not aware of any behavior of legitimate nodes and transmits radio jamming signals with its own strategy.

There are two key observations that drive our modeling of both reactive and non-reactive jammers. (1) In a time-critical application, a message becomes invalid as long as the message delay D is greater than its delay threshold σ. Thus, we define a metric, *message invalidation ratio*, to quantify the impact of jamming attacks against the time-critical application. (2) When a retransmission mechanism is adopted, to successfully disrupt the delivery of a time-critical message, the jammer needs to jam each transmission attempt of this message until the delay D is greater than σ. As a result, such behavior of the jammer is exactly the same as the behavior of *a gambler* who intends to win each play in a game to collect enough fortune to achieve his gambling goal of σ dollars.

Motivated by the two observations, we develop a gambling-based model to derive the message invalidation ratio of the time-critical application under jamming attacks. We validate our analysis and further evaluate the impact of jamming attacks on an experimental power substation network by examining a set of use cases specified by the National Institute of Standards and Technology (NIST). Based on theoretical and experimental results, we design the jamming attack detection based on estimation (JADE) system to achieve efficient and reliable jamming detection for the experimental substation network. Our contributions are threefold.

1. We introduce a new metric, message invalidation ratio, to quantify the performance of time-critical applications. Through theoretical and experimental studies, the message invalidation ratios are measured for a number of time-critical smart grid applications under a variety of jamming attacks.
2. For reactive jamming, we find that there exists a phase transition phenomenon of message delivery performance: when jamming probability p (the probability that a physical transmission is jammed) increases, the message invalidation ratio first increases slightly (and is negligible in practice), then increases dramatically to 1. For non-reactive jamming, there exists a similar phase transition phenomenon: when the average jamming interval (the time interval between two non-reactive jamming pulses) increases, the message invalidation ratio first has the value of 1, then decreases dramatically to 0.
3. Motivated by the phase transition phenomenon showing that a jammer only leads to negligible performance degradation when its jamming probability p is smaller than the transition point p^*, the proposed JADE method first estimates the jamming probability $\hat{p}$ and then compares $\hat{p}$ with p^* to detect jammers that can cause non-negligible impacts. JADE requires no online profiling/training step that is usually necessary in exiting methods [9, 12, 27]. We show via experiments that JADE achieves comparable detection performance with the statistically optimal likelihood ratio (LLR) test. We further show that JADE is more robust than the LLR test in the presence of a time-varying jammer.

The rest of this chapter is organized as follows. In Sect. 2.2, we describe preliminaries and the definition of message invalidation ratio. In Sects. 2.3 and 2.4, we model both reactive and non-reactive jamming attacks, derive the message invalidation ratios, and validate our analysis by performing experiments in a power substation network. In Sect. 2.5, we design and implement the JADE system for the substation network. Finally, we conclude in Sect. 2.6.

2.2 Models and Problem Statement

In this section, we first introduce the models of time-critical applications and jamming attacks, then define message invalidation ratio for later analysis.

Table 2.1 Time-critical message types in IEC 61850

Message type	Delay constraint (ms)	Purpose
Type 1A/P1	3	GOOSE trip protection
Type 1A/P2	10	GOOSE trip protection
Type 1B/P1	100	Automation system interaction
Type 1B/P2	20	Automation system interaction

2.2.1 Network and Traffic Models

As of today, the smart grid [19] has become one of the most important cyber-physical systems with a wide range of time-critical applications, we therefore focus on developing models for time-critical wireless networks with applications to the smart grid. Specifically, we consider a single-hop wireless network for a local-area system (e.g., a power substation in the smart grid [2, 11, 26]). The primary goal of such a network is to achieve efficient and reliable communication between local physical devices. There are two types of communication traffic in the network: time-critical and non-time-critical messages.

- Time-critical traffic is used for monitoring, control and protection of electronic devices on physical infrastructures. Such traffic has even more stringent timing requirements than conventional delay-sensitive traffic (e.g., video streaming on the Internet). For example, IEC 61850 [10] is a recent communication standard for power substation automation. IEC 61850 defines a variety of message types with specific timing constraints, in which the most time-critical message type, Generic Object Oriented Substation Event (GOOSE), shown in Table 2.1, has two end-to-end delay constraints[1]: 3 ms and 10 ms.
- Non-time-critical traffic is used for general-purpose exchange of system data, such as logging or file transferring [10]. Non-time-critical traffic usually does not have delay requirements. For example, IEC 61850 does not explicitly define the delay specification for substation non-critical file transferring, but suggests a timing requirement equal to or greater than 1000 ms.

We will focus on time-critical messages in this work. An example of transmitting such messages in smart grid applications is *raw data sampling* [10]: in a power distribution substation, an electronic device, called merging unit, keeps sampling the power signal on feeders, sends the sampled data to protection and control devices, which monitor the stream of sampled raw data and are programmed with incident protection procedures. The messages containing raw data samples are required to be delivered in 3 ms to ensure timely incident management. To transmit

---

[1]The end-to-end delay of a message is defined as the time interval from the instant that the transmitter's application layer generates the message to the instant that the receiver's application layer successfully receives it.

such time-critical messages, there are several fundamental requirements: (1) time-critical messages must be processed with the highest priority; (2) simple protocol processing and low communication overhead are required; (3) packet queuing or buffering should be avoided.

As a result, IEC 61850 maps the most time-critical GOOSE messages from the application layer directly to the MAC/link layer to reduce processing time and avoid tedious protocol headers. In this regard, since there is no transport layer to guarantee reliability, IEC 61850 defines that the application layer simply retransmits the same GOOSE message multiple times to ensure reliability.

Accordingly, we assume that a time-critical message with end-to-end delay constraint σ is passed from the application layer directly to the MAC layer. There is no flow and congestion control for the transmission. The application layer has a simple processing function that retransmits the same message after the previous transmission fails. But the application layer will stop retransmission once the message delay exceeds the constraint σ, since the message becomes obsolete or invalid. In addition, we assume that the time-critical network is always unsaturated (i.e., the network bandwidth is greater than the overall traffic load). Otherwise, the timing requirement of a time-critical message may not be guaranteed since the message has to be queued before transmission.

2.2.2   Jamming Models

The broadcast nature of wireless channels inevitably exposes time-critical wireless networks to jamming attacks that may severely degrade the network performance [3, 21, 27]. The jamming problem in conventional wireless network has been extensively studied regarding jamming strategies [3, 21, 27], jamming detection [9, 12, 25], and anti-jamming technologies [4, 13, 17, 20, 23, 24]. According to [27], we summarize wireless jamming attacks into two major types.

1. Reactive jammers, as shown in Fig. 2.1a. Reactive jammers [13, 20, 23, 27] are aware of the target communication systems. They stay quiet when the channel is idle, but start transmitting radio signals (or even meaningful signals [13]) to undermine ongoing communication as soon as they sense activity on the wireless channel.

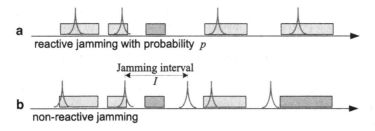

Fig. 2.1 Reactive jamming versus non-reactive jamming (**a**) reactive jamming behavior (**b**) non-reactive jamming behavior

2. Non-reactive jammers, as shown in Fig. 2.1b. Non-reactive jammers are not aware of any behavior of legitimate nodes and transmit the radio interference over the wireless channel following their own jamming strategies.

Reactive jammers disrupt legitimate transmissions in a more active and versatile manner than non-reactive jammers. When a reactive jammer senses an ongoing packet transmission, it can jam the packet with a controllable probability p. Thus, we model the strategy of a reactive jammer as follows.

Definition 2.1. The strategy of a reactive jammer is represented by $\mathscr{J}_r(p)$, where $p \in [0, 1]$ is the jamming probability, defined as the probability that a physical transmission can be successfully jammed.

Non-reactive jammers have no information of wireless channel activity, and transmit jamming pulse signals following a pre-defined pattern. Typical non-reactive jammers include periodical and random jammers in the literature [3, 27]. For a non-reactive jammer, the jamming interval I is an essential parameter [3] to characterize its behavior. If a jammer intends to disrupt more physical transmissions, it can use a very small jamming interval I. To the extreme, the non-reactive jammer with $I=0$ becomes a continuous jammer. Thus, we use the jamming interval I to model a non-reactive jammer and formally define its strategy as follows.

Definition 2.2. The strategy of a non-reactive jammer is represented by $\mathscr{J}_{nr}(I)$, where $I \geq 0$ is the jamming interval, defined as the time interval between two adjacent jamming pulses transmitted by the jammer.

The non-reactive jamming model in Definition 2.2 can represent several widely-used jamming models in the literature. For example, when the jamming interval I is a constant, the model becomes the periodic jamming model [3, 27]; when I is exponentially distributed, the model becomes the memoryless jamming model [3].

Although existing work (e.g. [3, 27]) has shown that a non-reactive jammer is less efficient than a reactive jammer, it is still an easy and simple way to disrupt legitimate traffic in wireless networks. Thus, we consider both reactive and non-reactive jammers in our jamming models.

2.2.3 Problem Statement

We have modeled the time-critical transmission mechanism and jamming strategies. We then define a performance metric to model the impact of jamming attacks on time-critical traffic.

In conventional networks, legitimate nodes usually request data services from service providers or exchange data among their neighbors. Hence, the throughput is an important performance metric in such networks. However, as stated earlier, the primary goal of time-critical wireless networks is to achieve efficient message delivery for reliable monitoring and control of a variety of physical infrastructures, instead of providing high throughput for clients. Hence, the delay performance of time-critical applications is of much more importance than the conventional throughput performance. A time-critical message becomes invalid as long as its message delay D is greater than the delay constraint σ. In order to directly reflect how a time-critical message can be delivered on time, we define a performance metric, message invalidation ratio, to evaluate the performance of time-critical applications.

Definition 2.3. For a time-critical message with delay constraint σ, the message invalidation ratio is defined as $r = \mathbb{P}\{D > \sigma\}$, where D is the end-to-end delay of the message.

As we can see, the message invalidation ratio is in fact the tail distribution of the message delay. Thus, for a time-critical application under jamming attacks, the derivation of delay distribution is equivalent to the derivation of message invalidation ratio. With the definition of message invalidation ratio, we formally state our problem of quantifying the impact of jamming attacks against time-critical traffic as follows.

Problem Statement In a time-critical wireless network, given a time-critical message with end-to-end delay constraint σ, find the message invalidation ratios of the time-critical message under jamming strategies $\mathscr{J}_r(p)$ and $\mathscr{J}_{nr}(I)$, respectively.

In following sections, we first use analytical modeling to derive the message invalidation ratio and perform real-time experiments in a power substation network to validate our analysis. Then, we present the design and experimental results of our jamming detection method.

2.3   Main Analytical Results

The key question in our study is to answer what is the time-critical message invalidation ratio under both reactive and non-reactive jamming attacks. Accordingly, we separate the question into two parts and investigate the message invalidation ratios with jamming strategies $\mathscr{J}_r(p)$ and $\mathscr{J}_{nr}(I)$, respectively.

2.3.1   Impact of Reactive Jamming with $\mathscr{J}_r(p)$

We first formulate the reactive jamming problem into a gambling problem, and then derive the message invalidation ratio of time-critical applications under jamming attacks.

Consider a transmitter that has a time-critical message to send with delay constraint σ, and a jammer with strategy $\mathscr{J}_r(p)$ that attempts to disrupt message delivery in the network. The process for the transmitter to send the time-critical

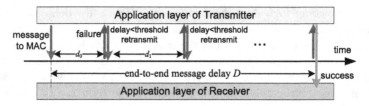

Fig. 2.2 Transmission process of time-critical messages at application layer

message is illustrated in Fig. 2.2: The time-critical message is initially generated at the application layer and is passed directly to the MAC layer to transmit. However, the transmission by the MAC layer may not succeed in the presence of the jammer. If transmission failure (e.g., ACK timeout) is reported by the MAC layer, the application layer will retransmit the same message as long as the cumulative message delay does not exceed the threshold σ. Therefore, the end-to-end message delay can be represented as

$$D = \sum_{i=0}^{N} d_i, \qquad (2.1)$$

where N is the number of retransmissions and d_i is the MAC-layer delay during the ith retransmission.

Note that the number of retransmissions N and the MAC-layer delay d_i are both random variables due to the random backoff mechanism used in wireless MAC protocol (e.g., WiFi and Zigbee). If a message has no delay constraint, the application layer will keep transmitting the same message until it succeeds. In this case, the number of retransmissions N follows the geometric distribution. Then, the end-to-end delay D in (2.1) becomes a geometric sum and it is not difficult to use asymptotic analysis to derive the distribution of D, similarly to existing work on computing the delay distribution for CSMA/CA networks (e.g., [3, 16]).

However, in our case with a specific delay threshold σ, jamming attacks can only lead to a finite number of retransmissions at the application layer. The number of retransmissions N is in fact a bounded random variable dynamically coupled with the sum of MAC-layer delays $\{d_i\}$, since every time the application layer compares the accumulated message delay with the constraint σ to check whether it should resend a transmission-failed message or drop it. Consequently, it is non-trivial to accurately model and derive the message invalidation ratio of the time-critical application under jamming attacks.

We then take a closer look at the transmission process for a time-critical message. There are two key observations.

1. Such a process has only two outcomes: the jammer either wins or loses. That is, either the jammer keeps successfully jamming every transmission until the delay is larger than the threshold, or the transmitter successfully delivers the message within the timing constraint.

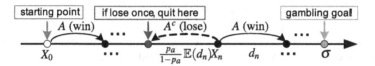

Fig. 2.3 Setups of our gambling game: the gambler either wins d_n dollars (event A) or loses $\frac{p_a}{1-p_a}\mathbb{E}(d_n)$ dollars (event A^c) in the nth play. The gambler quits when he either reaches his gambling goal or loses once

2. In order to win, the jammer must cumulatively collect the reward, i.e., message delay. Every time he jams a physical transmission, a certain amount of delay contributes to the overall message delay.

Is there any process satisfying the two properties? Yes, it is *gambling*. In other words, if we consider the jammer as a gambler and the delay as money, we can exactly map our problem into a gambling game: a gambler attempts to win a game by consistently winning money to reach his goal. The probabilistic modeling of a gambling game, such as the *gambler's ruin* problem [6], has been well investigated by mathematicians. It has been shown that martingale theory [6], a branch of modern probabilistic measure theory, is an effective tool to solve the *gambler's ruin* problem. Therefore, we are motivated to map our problem into a gambling game and solve it by using martingale theory.

We first construct a game for a gambler shown in Fig. 2.3. The gambler starts with $X_0 = d_0$ dollars. In the nth play, when event A happens (with probability p_a), the gambler wins d_n dollars; when event A^c happens (with probability $1 - p_a$), he loses $\frac{p_a}{1-p_a}\mathbb{E}(d_n)$ dollars.[2] His gambling goal is σ dollars. The gambler quits when he either reaches his gambling goal or loses once (i.e., A^c happens).

Let $\{X_n\}$ be the gambler's money in the nth play. Specifically, we can write X_n as follows.

$$X_0 = d_0, \quad X_n = X_{n-1} + \xi_n, \quad (n \in \mathbb{N}), \tag{2.2}$$

where $\mathbb{N}$ is the set of positive integers, ξ_n is the reward for the gambler in the nth play. Since the gambler can either win or lose in the nth play, the reward ξ_n can be written as

$$\xi_n = d_n \mathbf{1}_A - \frac{p_a}{1 - p_a}\mathbb{E}(d_n)\mathbf{1}_{A^c}, \tag{2.3}$$

where $\mathbf{1}_A$ is the indicator function, defined as

$$\mathbf{1}_A = \begin{cases} 1 & \text{event } A \text{ happens,} \\ 0 & \text{event } A^c \text{ happens.} \end{cases} \tag{2.4}$$

---

[2] The value of $\frac{p_a}{1-p_a}\mathbb{E}(d_n)$ does not affect the interpretation of our gambling game mapping. It will be shown later that this value is essential to our martingale construction.

Then, we map our scenario of the time-critical transmission into the gambling game: the jammer is the gambler and the delay is money. Each transmission can be regarded as a play. Let event $A = \{$the gambler wins money in a play$\} = \{$transmission failure at the MAC layer$\}$. The goal of the jammer/gambler is to make the delay/money larger than the threshold σ. To achieve this goal, the jammer/gambler must keep jamming/winning successfully in each transmission/play (i.e., event A always happens). However, once A^c happens, the gambler/jammer loses/fails (i.e., the message is successfully delivered within the delay constraint σ). The message invalidation ratio, which denotes the probability that the cumulative delay is larger than the threshold, is equivalent to the probability that the gambler reaches his goal before he loses.

Note that p_a denotes the transmission failure probability at the MAC layer. Since wireless MAC usually has its own retransmission mechanism due to CSMA/CA (e.g., the default long and short retry limits in IEEE 802.11g are 3 and 7, respectively), event A happens only when every MAC-layer transmission attempt is disrupted by the jammer. Thus, given the number of MAC layer transmission attempts N_{mac}, we obtain $p_a = p^{N_{mac}}$. Since it has been shown (e.g.,[1]) that the collision probability due to legitimate traffic is small if the network is unsaturated, we neglect the impact of legitimate traffic on the MAC-layer transmission failure in our analysis. (We will consider the impact in experiments later).

We have set up the rules for our gambling game. We then use the gambling-based model to derive the message invalidation ratio of time-critical applications under jamming attacks. Before we proceed, we first present the definition of a martingale according to [6].

Definition 2.4 (Martingale). A process $\{X_n\}$ is called a martingale relative to a filtration $\{\mathscr{F}_n\}$, (A sequence of σ-algebras $\{\mathscr{F}_n\}$ is called a filtration if $\mathscr{F}_n \subset \mathscr{F}_{n+1}$ for any $n \in \mathbb{N}$.) if (1) X_n is $\mathscr{F}_n$-measurable, (2) $\mathbb{E}|X_n| < \infty$ for any $n \in \mathbb{N}$, (3) $\mathbb{E}(X_n|\mathscr{F}_{n-1}) = X_{n-1}$ almost surely.

We then show that the gambler's money $\{X_n\}$ is in fact a martingale due to our construction.

Lemma 2.1. *The process $\{X_n\}$ defined in (2.2) is a martingale.*

Proof. We prove $\{X_n\}$ is a martingale by verifying the definition.

(i) It is obvious from our construction that $\{X_n\}$ is relative to a filtration $\{\mathscr{F}_n\}$ and X_n is $\mathscr{F}_n$-measurable.

(ii) For any $n \in N$, we have $\mathbb{E}|X_n| = \mathbb{E}|X_0 + \sum_{i=1}^{n} \xi_i| \le \mathbb{E}|X_0| + n\mathbb{E}|\xi_i|$. Then, it suffices to show $\mathbb{E}|\xi_i| < \infty$. Observe that

$$\mathbb{E}|\xi_i| = \mathbb{E}|d_i \mathbf{1}_A - \frac{p_a}{1-p_a} \mathbb{E}(d_i)\mathbf{1}_{A^c}| \le \mathbb{E}|d_i| + \frac{p_a}{1-p_a}\mathbb{E}|d_i| < \infty. \quad (2.5)$$

for $0 < p_a < 1$. We obtain $\mathbb{E}|X_n| < \infty$ for $0 < p_a < 1$.

(iii) Then, we prove $\mathbb{E}(X_n|\mathscr{F}_{n-1}) = X_{n-1}$. First, for any i, it holds that

$$\mathbb{E}(\xi_i) = \mathbb{E}(d_i \mathbf{1}_A - \frac{p_a}{1-p_a}\mathbb{E}(d_i)\mathbf{1}_{A^c})$$

$$= p_a\mathbb{E}(d_i) - \frac{p_a}{1-p_a}(1-p_a)\mathbb{E}(d_i) = 0. \tag{2.6}$$

Then, we have

$$\mathbb{E}(X_n|\mathscr{F}_{n-1}) = \mathbb{E}(X_{n-1} + \xi_n|\mathscr{F}_{n-1}) = X_{n-1} + \mathbb{E}(\xi_n|\mathscr{F}_{n-1})$$

$$= X_{n-1} + \mathbb{E}(\xi_n) = X_{n-1}. \tag{2.7}$$

From (i), (ii), and (iii), we obtain $\{X_n\}$ is a martingale. □

We then present our main result of the message invalidation ratio for time-critical traffic under jamming attacks.

Theorem 2.1 (Message Invalidation Ratio for General Cases). *Given a jamming strategy $\mathscr{J}_r(p)$, the message invalidation ratio r is*

$$r = \frac{\mathbb{E}(D_s) - \frac{c}{1-p_a}}{\mathbb{E}(D_s) - \frac{p_a c}{1-p_a} - \mathbb{E}(D_u)}, \tag{2.8}$$

where $p_a = p^{N_{mac}}$, $c = \mathbb{E}(d_i)$ is the mean of the i.i.d. MAC-layer delay d_i, $D_s \leq \sigma$ is the end-to-end delay of a successfully delivered message, and $D_u > \sigma$ is the delay of failed message delivery, defined as the interval from the instant that the transmitter starts transmitting a message to the instant that the transmitter stops retransmission due to message invalidation.[3]

Proof. Let $n_1 = \inf_{n\in\mathbb{N}}\{X_n < X_{n-1}\}$. According to our construction, event $\{X_n < X_{n-1}\}$ happens if and only if $\xi_n < 0$ (i.e., event A^c happens at the nth play). Therefore, n_1 is the minimum time at which the gambler loses money (or, a transmission succeeds).

Let $n_2 = \inf_{n\in\mathbb{N}}\{X_n > \sigma\}$. Then, n_2 is the minimum time at which the gambler reaches his goal (or, the message delay is larger than the threshold).

Thus, $\{n_1 > n_2\}$ means that event $\{X_n < X_{n-1}\}$ never happens prior to event $\{X_n > \sigma\}$, or the gambler reaches his gambling goal without any loss in each play. In other words, event $\{n_1 > n_2\}$ means that the jammer successfully delays the transmission of a message and leads to invalidation of the message.

Therefore, the message invalidation ratio $r = \mathbb{P}(n_1 > n_2)$. Let $n_{\text{stop}} = \min(n_1, n_2)$. Then, n_{stop} is a bounded stopping time and

$$X_{n_{\text{stop}}} = X_{n_1}\mathbf{1}_{\{n_1 < n_2\}} + X_{n_2}\mathbf{1}_{\{n_1 > n_2\}}, \tag{2.9}$$

---

[3] Note that the reason for $D_u > \sigma$ is that the MAC layer still needs to finish an ongoing transmission even though the application layer is aware that the cumulative delay exceeds the constant σ.

where X_{n_1} denotes the remaining money after the gambler loses money for the first time. Then, X_{n_1-1} denotes the money before the gambler loses his money, which is exactly the end-to-end delay of successful message delivery D_s. Thus,

$$X_{n_1} = X_{n_1-1} - \frac{p_a \mathbb{E}(d_{n_1})}{1-p_a} = D_s - \frac{p_a c}{1-p_a}. \tag{2.10}$$

On the other hand, X_{n_2} denotes the money after the gambler achieves his gambling goal of σ dollars and quits. Thus, X_{n_2} is exactly the delay of failed message delivery:

$$X_{n_2} = D_u. \tag{2.11}$$

Since $\{X_n\}$ is a martingale (from Lemma 2.1) and n_{stop} is a bounded stopping time, we obtain from Doob's optional sampling theorem [6, Ch. 10] that the mean value of a martingale $\{X_n\}$ at a stopping time n_{stop} is equal to the mean value at the starting point 0; i.e.,

$$\mathbb{E}(X_{n_{\text{stop}}}) = \mathbb{E}(X_0). \tag{2.12}$$

Then, it follows from (2.9) and (2.12) that

$$\mathbb{E}(X_{n_{\text{stop}}}) = \mathbb{E}(X_{n_1})\mathbb{P}(n_1 < n_2) + \mathbb{E}(X_{n_2})\mathbb{P}(n_1 > n_2)$$
$$= (1-r)(\mathbb{E}(D_s) - p_a c/(1-p_a)) + r\mathbb{E}(D_u) = \mathbb{E}(X_0) = \mathbb{E}(d_0). \tag{2.13}$$

Therefore, we obtain from (2.13) that

$$r = \frac{\mathbb{E}(D_s) - \frac{c}{1-p_a}}{\mathbb{E}(D_s) - \frac{p_a c}{1-p_a} - \mathbb{E}(D_u)} \tag{2.14}$$

$\square$

Theorem 2.1 shows that the message invalidation ratio can be analytically represented only by first-order statistics. The result in Theorem 2.1 is general since it does not make further assumptions on the distribution of the MAC-layer delay. To illustrate intuitive relations between message invalidation ratio r, jamming probability p, and delay threshold σ, we present our complementary analytical result as follows.

Theorem 2.2 (General Upper Bound). *For the message invalidation ratio r in Theorem 2.1, it satisfies that*

$$r \leq \frac{p^{N_{mac}} c}{(1-p^{N_{mac}})(\sigma - c) + p^{N_{mac}} c}.$$

Proof. From Theorem 2.1, we have

$$r = \frac{\mathbb{E}(D_s) - \frac{c}{1-p_a}}{\mathbb{E}(D_s) - \frac{p_a c}{1-p_a} - \mathbb{E}(D_u)} = 1 - \frac{\mathbb{E}(D_u) - c}{\mathbb{E}(D_u) + \frac{p_a c}{1-p_a} - \mathbb{E}(D_s)}$$

$$\leq 1 - \frac{\mathbb{E}(D_u) - c}{\mathbb{E}(D_u) + \frac{p_a c}{1-p_a} - c} = \frac{\frac{p_a c}{1-p_a}}{\mathbb{E}(D_u) + \frac{p_a c}{1-p_a} - c}. \tag{2.15}$$

Since the delay of failed message delivery D_u is always larger than σ ($D_u \geq \sigma$), it follows from (2.15) that

$$r \leq \frac{\frac{p_a c}{1-p_a}}{\sigma + \frac{p_a c}{1-p_a} - c} = \frac{p_a c}{(1-p_a)(\sigma - c) + p_a c}. \tag{2.16}$$

Since $p_a = p_{mac}^N$, we finally obtain from (2.16) that

$$r \leq \frac{p^{N_{mac}} c}{(1 - p^{N_{mac}})(\sigma - c) + p^{N_{mac}} c}. \tag{2.17}$$

$\square$

Remark 2.1. Theorem 2.2 provides a general upper bound of message invalidation ratio for time-critical applications. Note that when the jamming probability p is sufficiently small, $(1 - p^{N_{mac}})(\sigma - c) \approx \sigma - c \gg p^{N_{mac}} c$. We obtain that the upper bound of r in (2.17) can be approximated as $p^{N_{mac}} c/(\sigma - c)$, indicating that the message invalidation ratio decays at least polynomially when p is small and decreasing to 0. Consequently, a small jamming probability p cannot lead to significant impact on the performance of time-critical applications.

Example 2.1. Figure 2.4 numerically illustrates the upper bound of the message invalidation ratio for a time-critical application with $10\,\text{ms} < \sigma < 100\,\text{ms}$, $N_{mac} = 3$, and $c = \mathbb{E}(d_i) = 1\,\text{ms}$ under the attack of a reactive jammer with $0 < p < 1$. We observe from Fig. 2.4 that the message invalidation ratio, as a function of jamming probability p, has a phase transition phenomenon. That is, as p increases, the message invalidation ratio has two distinct increasing phases: a slightly-increasing phase and a dramatically-increasing phase. For example, when $\sigma = 10\,\text{ms}$, the transition point is approximately at $p = 0.7$ and the corresponding upper bound of message invalidation ratio is $r = 5\,\%$. In other words, the upper bound only increases from $0\,\%$ slightly to $5\,\%$ as p goes from 0 to 0.7 and increases from $5\,\%$ dramatically to $100\,\%$ as p goes from 0.7 to 1.

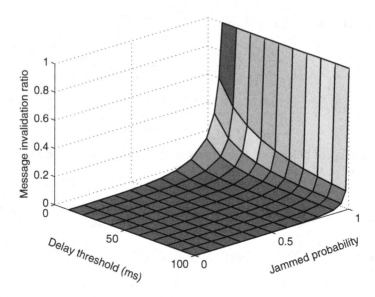

Fig. 2.4 Upper bound of message invalidation ratio for a time-critical application under reactive jamming

2.3.2   Impact of Non-reactive Jamming with $\mathscr{J}_{nr}(I)$

We next present our main results of the impact of non-reactive jamming on time-critical messages. For a non-reactive jammer with $\mathscr{J}_{nr}(I)$, its jamming interval I can be arbitrarily chosen to adopt various jamming patterns. Since it may be impractical to use one model to include all possible non-reactive jamming patterns, we considered two non-reactive jamming models that are widely-adopted in the literature [3, 27]: memoryless jamming (I is exponentially distributed) and periodic jamming (I is a constant).

By taking advantage of our previous result in Theorem 2.2, we have the following results for the two widely-used types of non-reactive jamming.

Proposition 2.1. *For a non-reactive jamming strategy $\mathscr{J}_{nr}(I)$,*

(i) if I is exponentially distributed, the message invalidation ratio r can be upper-bounded by

$$r \le \frac{c(1 - e^{-L\mathbb{E}(I)})^{N_{mac}}}{(1 - (\sigma - c)(1 - e^{-L\mathbb{E}(I)})^{N_{mac}}) + c(1 - e^{-L\mathbb{E}(I)})^{N_{mac}}}. \qquad (2.18)$$

where $c = \mathbb{E}(d_i)$, L is the packet length (measured in time).

(ii) If I is a constant, the message invalidation ratio r can be approximated as

$$
r \approx \begin{cases}
1 & I \le L \\
(1-\frac{\sigma(I-L)}{IL})\mathbf{1}_{\{2L\le\sigma<\frac{IL}{I-L}\}}+\frac{L}{I}\mathbf{1}_{\{\sigma<2L\}} & L<I<2L \\
\frac{L}{I}\mathbf{1}_{\{\sigma<2L\}} & I>2L,
\end{cases} \tag{2.19}
$$

where L is the packet length.

Proof. The proof consists of two parts.

(i) As the jamming interval between two adjacent jamming pulses is exponentially distributed, the probability that a jamming signal is generated during the physical transmission of a packet is $1-e^{-L\mathbb{E}(I)}$. Since exponential distribution is memoryless, the jamming probability for each physical transmission is always $1-e^{-L\mathbb{E}(I)}$. Thus, the memoryless jammer with strategy $J_{nr}(I)$ is equivalent to a reactive jammer with strategy $J_r(p)$, where $p=1-e^{-L\mathbb{E}(I)}$. By using Theorem 2.2, we obtain

$$
r \le p^{N_{\mathrm{mac}}}c/((1-p^{N_{\mathrm{mac}}})(\sigma-c)+p^{N_{\mathrm{mac}}}c)
$$
$$
\le \frac{c(1-e^{-L\mathbb{E}(I)})^{N_{\mathrm{mac}}}}{(1-(\sigma-c)(1-e^{-L\mathbb{E}(I)})^{N_{\mathrm{mac}}})+c(1-e^{-L\mathbb{E}(I)})^{N_{\mathrm{mac}}}}. \tag{2.20}
$$

(ii) When I is a constant, the jammer is a periodic one. It is evident that when the jamming interval $I \le L$, every physical transmission will be jammed, since there exists at least one jamming pulse during one transmission as shown in Fig. 2.5. Hence, we have

$$
\mathbb{P}(\text{message is invalid}|I \le L) = 1. \tag{2.21}
$$

When $I > L$, define event $B_i = \{$the ith transmission is jammed$\}$. Consider the first transmission and event B_1, since the transmission and jamming processing are independent, $\mathbb{P}(B_1)$ is equivalent to the probability that there is not jamming pulse over a first transmission interval of L. Thus, $\mathbb{P}(B_1) = L/I$. The message

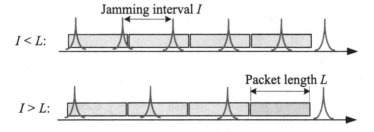

Fig. 2.5 Diagram of periodic jammers with intervals $I \le L$ and $I > L$

invalidation probability can be represented as

$$\mathbb{P}(\text{message is invalid}) = \mathbb{P}\left(\cap_{i=1}^{\sigma/L} B_i\right). \tag{2.22}$$

When $\sigma < 2L$ and the first transmission fails, even the second transmission succeeds, the message will still become invalid; therefore the message invalidation ratio depends only on the first transmission results. We then have

$$\mathbb{P}(\text{message is invalid}|I > L, \sigma < 2L) = \mathbb{P}(B_1) = I/L. \tag{2.23}$$

When $\sigma \geq 2L$ and $I \geq 2L$, the second transmission always succeeds. Then,

$$\mathbb{P}(\text{message is invalid}|I \geq 2L, \sigma \geq 2L) = 0. \tag{2.24}$$

When $\sigma \geq 2L$ and $L < I < 2L$, the transmitter can make approximately σ/L transmission attempts to send the message. The jammer must jam all these transmission in order to disrupt the message delivery. Since the periodic jammer transmits pulses at a constant rate, events $\{B_i\}$ are dependent. We in the following use deduction to obtain the result for this case.

As shown in Fig. 2.6, if the first transmission arrives between times a and a_1 ($a_1 = a + (I - L)$), there will be no jamming during the transmission. Then, the first transmission will be jammed if and only if it arrives between times a_1 and b. However this time interval can only guarantee the first transmission to be jammed. If the first transmission arrives between times a_1 and a_2 ($a_2 = a_1 + (I - L)$), there will be no jamming during the second transmission. Therefore, the first and second transmissions will be both jammed if and only if the first transmission arrives between times a_2 and b.

By using deduction, we obtain that all σ/L transmissions will be jammed if and only if the first transmission arrives between times $a_{\sigma/L}$ and b, where $a_{\sigma/L} = a + \sigma(I - L)/L$ and $b = a + I$. If $a_{\sigma/L} \geq b$, there always exists a transmission, during which there is no jamming pulse. Thus, we have

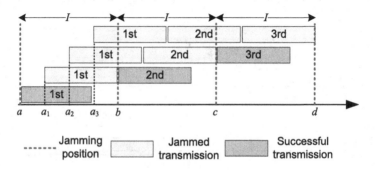

Fig. 2.6 Diagram of periodic jamming with $\sigma \geq 2L$ and $L < I < 2L$

$$\mathbb{P}(\text{message is invalid}|\sigma \geq IL/(I-L), L<I<2L) = 0. \tag{2.25}$$

Otherwise, the message invalidation ratio is

$$\mathbb{P}(\text{message is invalid}|\sigma \geq IL/(I-L), L<I<2L)$$
$$= \mathbb{P}(\text{first transmission arrives at } [a_{\frac{\sigma}{L}}, b])$$
$$= (I - \sigma(I-L)/L)/I = 1 - \sigma(I-L)/(IL). \tag{2.26}$$

Combining (2.21), (2.23)–(2.26) yields the results of the impact of periodic jamming. $\square$

Example 2.2 (Memoryless Jamming). Figure 2.7 numerically illustrates the upper bound of the message invalidation ratio for a time-critical application with 5 ms $<\sigma<$ 20 ms, $N_{mac} = 3$, $L = 0.5$ ms, and $c = \mathbb{E}(d_i) = 2$ ms under the attack of a memoryless jammer with 0 ms $<\mathbb{E}(I)<$ 0.04 ms. Different from Fig. 2.4, Fig. 2.7 shows that the message invalidation ratio consists of three decreasing phases: as the average jamming interval $\mathbb{E}(I)$ increases from 0, the message invalidation first remains 1, then dramatically decreases, and finally approaches 0.

Example 2.3 (Periodic Jamming). Figure 2.8 numerically illustrates the message invalidation ratio for a time-critical application with 1 ms $<\sigma<$ 20 ms and $L = 0.5$ ms under the attack of a periodic jammer with 0 ms $<I<$ 1 ms. Similar to Fig. 2.7, Fig. 2.8 shows that the message invalidation ratio also consists of three decreasing

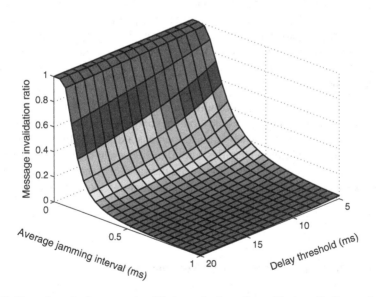

Fig. 2.7 Upper bound of message invalidation ratio for a time-critical application under non-reactive memoryless jamming

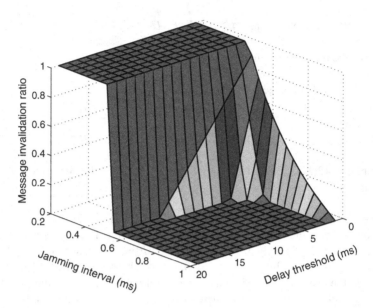

Fig. 2.8 The approximate message invalidation ratio for a time-critical application under non-reactive periodic jamming

phases: as the jamming interval I increases from 0, the message invalidation first remains 1, then sharply decreases, and finally approaches 0.

Figures 2.7 and 2.8 show that for non-reactive jamming, there always exists two critical values I_1 and I_2: If $\mathbb{E}(I) < I_1$, non-reactive jammers can almost disrupt all time-critical transmissions. If $\mathbb{E}(I) > I_2$, non-reactive jammers only cause negligible effect on time-critical transmission. Due to randomness, a memoryless jammer's message invalidation ratio transition region from 1 to 0 is much smoother than a periodic jammer.

Remark 2.2. From our analytical results, we summarize that for reactive jamming with $\mathscr{J}_r(p)$, there exists a phase transition phenomenon: the message invalidation ratio first has a slightly increase phase and then has a dramatically increase phase, as the jamming probability p increases from 0 to 1. For non-reactive jamming with $\mathscr{J}_{nr}(I)$, the message invalidation ratio first has the value of 1, then has a dramatically decreasing phase and finally approaches 0 as the jamming interval I increases from 0 to infinity.

2.4 Experimental Study in Power Networks

We have so far derived analytical results for a time-critical application under both reactive and non-reactive jamming attacks. Next, we perform extensive experiments to further investigate the jamming impact on time-critical wireless networks.

Fig. 2.9 The enhanced retransmission mechanism in GOOSE

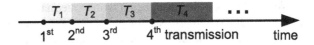

As aforementioned, there are a few existing works [5, 7, 11, 28] that have shown the advantage and efficiency of wireless networks for the smart grid based on off-the-shelf wireless products (e.g., WiFi and CDMA). In this section, we use real-time experiments to show quantitatively to what extent jamming attacks can cause damages to a practical wireless network for smart grid applications.

2.4.1 Experimental Setups

As IEC 61850 [10] is a recent smart grid communication standard for power substations, we choose IEC 61850 as our power communication protocol. Since GOOSE messages in IEC 61850 have very strict timing requirements, we use different GOOSE applications to evaluate the impact of jamming attacks on a wireless network. Specifically, we consider two protocol-defined GOOSE applications: Types 1A/P1 and 1A/P2 with constraints of 3 ms and 10 ms [10], respectively. We also consider two GOOSE applications for transfer trip protection and anti-islanding with delay constraints of 8–16 ms and 150–300 ms [11], respectively.

The GOOSE application layer features an enhanced retransmission mechanism [10], in which the same message is retransmitted with increasing retransmission intervals. As shown in Fig. 2.9, the first retransmission interval is T_1, the second one is $T_2 \geq T_1$, and the interval keeps increasing up to T_{max}. How T_1 increases to T_{max} is claimed to be a local issue and is not standardized in IEC 61850. Therefore, the interval of each retransmission is increased equally by δ in our implementation.

We set up a WiFi-based wireless power network to evaluate the GOOSE performance under jamming attacks. Since GOOSE is mapped from the application layer directly to the MAC layer, we implement a GOOSE messaging module in the Linux kernel. Detailed setups are as follows.

1. Protocols: IEC 61850 GOOSE over WiFi.
2. GOOSE parameters: we set $T_1 = 1$ ms, $T_{max} = 5$ ms, and $\delta = 1$ ms. For the most time-critical (3 ms) case, we set $T_1 = T_{max} = 1$ ms. During the experiments, the application layer is set to stop retransmission once the message delay exceeds the threshold.
3. WiFi parameters: IEEE 802.11g (ad-hoc mode) at 2.462 GHz. As GOOSE requires the highest priority for processing, we use the Madwifi driver [15] to set minimum and maximum 802.11 contention windows to be 4 and 8, respectively. We also set the retry limit to be 3.
4. Jammer: We use the USRP system with GNU radio (version 3.3) [8] to set up a low-power jammer to disrupt the GOOSE messaging. The jammer is programmed to be one of three types: reactive, memoryless, and periodic jammers. The length of jamming signals is set to be 22 μs as given in [3].

We use the message invalidation ratio to measure the jamming impact. We transmit 1000 GOOSE messages for every GOOSE application in each experiment, We then measure the delay of each GOOSE message, compare the delay with the threshold and compute the message invalidation ratio.

2.4.2 A Small-Scale Network Scenario

We now consider a WiFi-based power network scenario [22]: a transformer bay in a Type D2-1 power substation has two breaker intelligent electronic devices (IEDs), two protection-and-control (P&C) IEDs, and one merging-unit (MU) IED. All breaker IEDs and P&C IEDs periodically send updated meter values to a station server at a fixed rate of 20 Hz. The MU IED periodically sends raw data messages to P&C IEDs at a rate of 920 Hz, 2400 Hz, or 4800 Hz. (All setups are from [22].) Note that all traffic rates are measured at the application layer. We do not control the message transmission mechanism below the application layer. In fact, since we use the 802.11 MAC layer, the real traffic on the wireless channel may not be strictly periodic due to scheduling, backoff, and jamming. Our goal is to not only investigate the impact of jamming attacks but also evaluate the effect of legitimate traffic on GOOSE messaging in a small-scale power network over WiFi access.

We first evaluate the impact of a reactive jammer. Figures 2.10 and 2.11 show the message invalidation ratios of Type-1A/P1 (3 ms limit) and Type-1A/P2 (10 ms limit) GOOSE messages transmitted from a breaker IED to a P&C IED, respectively. Note that the WiFi-based network is always unsaturated even when the transmission rate of the MU IED is 4800 Hz. We can see from Figs. 2.10 and 2.11 that unsaturated traffic load has nearly negligible effect on the message invalidation ratio. For example, when the jamming probability p is fixed to be 0.8, the message invalidation ratio of Type-1A/P2 (10 ms limit) GOOSE messages increases from 4.9 to 5.2 % as the MU IED transmission rate goes from 920 to 4800 Hz.

We next investigate the impact of non-reactive jammers on the same network. Figure 2.12 shows the impact of a periodic jammer on Type-1A/P2 (10 ms limit) GOOSE messages transmitted from a breaker IED to a P&C IED. We observe from Fig. 2.12 that for the periodic jammer, increasing unsaturated traffic load also has negligible effect on the message invalidation ratio. For example, when the jamming interval $I = 0.2$ ms, the message invalidation only increases by 0.03 as the raw data sampling rate goes from 920 to 4800 Hz.

For our experiential results in Figs. 2.10, 2.11, and 2.12, we conclude that the increasing of unsaturated traffic load can only slightly degrade the performance of time-critical transmissions. It is also noted from Figs. 2.10, 2.11, and 2.12 that legitimate traffic does not affect the phase transition phenomenon of the message invalidation ratio. As a result, from the perspective of network performance evaluation, channel collision due to legitimate traffic can be regarded as a form of reactive jamming with small very jamming probability p, which has been shown to cause negligible impacts on time-critical transmission in both theoretical modeling and real-time experiments.

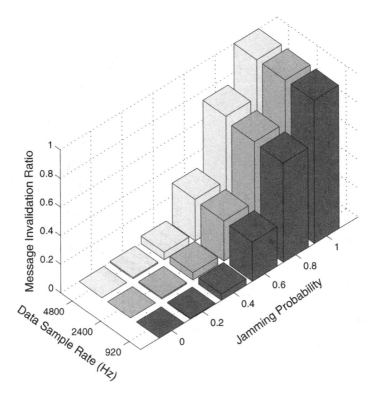

Fig. 2.10 Message invalidation ratio (Type-1A/P1 GOOSE with 3 ms limit) versus reactive jamming probability p and transmission rate of the MU IED

2.5   JADE: Jamming Attack Detection Based on Estimation

In previous sections, we have modeled the impact of jamming attacks on time-critical applications and validated our analysis by performing experiments in a power network. Our analytical and experimental results provide a prerequisite to the design of jamming detectors for wireless smart grid applications. In this section, we implement a jamming detection system, JADE (Jamming Attack Detection based on Estimation) to achieve both efficiency and reliability in wireless applications in a power substation.

2.5.1   Design and Implementation

Due to the importance of power networks, a jamming detector should yield a reliable output within a short decision time to notify network operators of potential threats. Existing methods in general require an online profiling step, which periodically

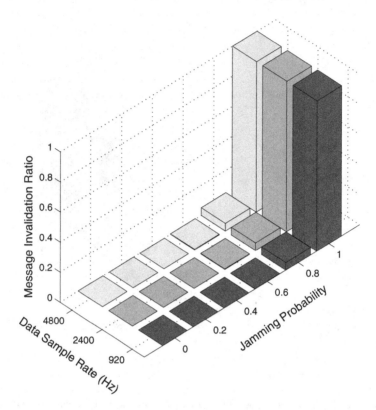

Fig. 2.11 Message invalidation ratio (Type-1A/P2 GOOSE with 10 ms limit) versus reactive jamming probability p and transmission rate of the MU IED

estimate parameters [12, 27] or infer statistical models [9, 25] from measured data, to provide empirical knowledge for jamming detection. For example, a sequential jamming detector proposed in [12] needs to estimate the transmission failure probabilities in both non-jamming and jamming cases before performing jamming detection. However, such profiling-based methods face several practical issues for time-critical systems: (1) the profiling phase inevitably increases the detection time; (2) it is unclear in practice how much reliability the profiling phase can provide for later jamming detection.

As we can see, existing profiling-based detectors may not be directly used in practical power systems. Thus, we are motivated to design a new jamming detection system, JADE, to achieve reliability for jamming detection in power systems as well as to shorten the decision time, compared with existing profiling-based methods. The intuition of JADE is as follows.

First, the online profiling based methods are used in ad-hoc or sensor networks where network parameters for a node (e.g., number of nodes, background traffic) are usually considered unknown. Therefore, online profiling is essential for jamming

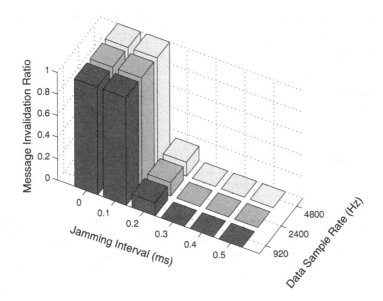

Fig. 2.12 Message invalidation ratio (Type-1A/P2 GOOSE with 10 ms limit) versus periodic jamming interval *I* and transmission rate of the MU IED

detection to accommodate changes of network setups and topologies. However, nodes in a power network are usually static and have nearly predictable traffic (e.g., the raw data sampling rate and meter update rate of IEDs). Thus, on-line profiling is not necessary, and off-line profiling should be sufficient for jamming detection in a power network. In other words, the profiling can be done during the network initialization or maintenance period, thereby shortening the decision time by eliminating (or significantly reducing the frequency of) the online profiling process.

Second, the goal of both reactive and non-reactive jammers is to disrupt the message delivery by jamming packets. Thus, there always exists a jamming-induced probability, denoting the probability that a packet will be disrupted by jamming. In this regard, every jammer can be considered as a reactive jammer with certain jamming probability p. As we observed previously, the phase transition phenomenon for the reactive jamming case indicates that when the jamming probability p is sufficiently small, the jamming impact is nearly negligible. This means that in order to detect the presence of a harmful jammer, a detection system only needs to estimate the jamming probability $\hat{p}$, and then to compare the estimation with a critical jamming probability p^*, with which a jammer can cause non-negligible impact on power networks. If $\hat{p}$ is small, whether it is induced by channel collision, fading, or even jamming, it cannot lead to significant performance degradation. Otherwise, the detection system should raise an alarm.

Algorithm 1 : A Single-Round Detection in JADE

Given: Threshold p^*, Number of needed samples N.
Initialization: $n \leftarrow 0, \hat{p} \leftarrow 0$.
repeat
    Transmit a packet and $n \leftarrow n + 1$.
    if transmission failure **then**
        $\hat{p} \leftarrow ((n-1) * \hat{p} + 1)/n$
    else
        $\hat{p} \leftarrow (n-1) * \hat{p}/n$
    end if
until n is equal to N
If $\hat{p} > p^*$, **print** Jamming Alarm.

Accordingly, we implement the JADE system at a MU IED that periodically transmits raw data samples at the rate of 920 Hz [11]. JADE observes the transmission result of each data sample and estimates the jamming probability $\hat{p}$ by

$$\hat{p} = \frac{1}{N} \sum_{i=1}^{N} 1_{F_i}, \qquad (2.27)$$

where N is the number of observations, and F_i denotes the event that the ith transmission fails.

After the estimation in (2.27), JADE raises a jamming alarm if $\hat{p} > p^*$. Detailed setups of JADE are shown in Algorithm 1. The threshold p^* can be chosen via offline profiling (i.e., via either theoretical analysis or experiments). In particular, as aforementioned, nodes in a power network are usually static and have nearly predictable network traffic for monitoring and control. In other words, network setups including the number of nodes, network topology, traffic rates and timing requirements are all known to the network operator. In this regard, the threshold p^* can be chosen after the message invalidation ratio, as a function of jamming probability p, is computed. The choice of p^* can be further verified and adjusted by experiments during network setup and maintenance periods.

Note that when JADE transmits a message, it will use a time counter to measure the time when the ACK returns. If the ACK never returns and the counter reaches the timeout, JADE will conclude the transmission fails.

2.5.2 Experimental Results

We then use the experimental power network in Sect. 2.4.2 to assess the performance of JADE. As the lowest bound of GOOSE delay is 3 ms, we choose the corresponding critical jamming probability (detection threshold) $p^* = 0.3$ from experimental results in Fig. 2.10. We also implement the statistically optimal likelihood ratio (LLR) test in our experiments for performance comparison. (A sequential version

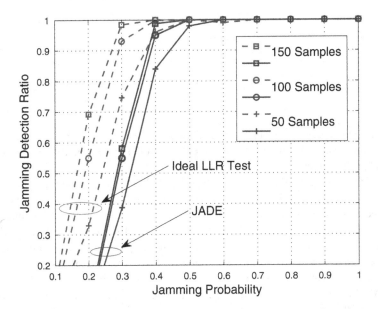

Fig. 2.13 Jamming detection ratios of both JADE and the likelihood ratio test in the presence of a jammer with different jamming probabilities

of the LLR test is used in [12].) The LLR test first requires a profiling step to estimate the packet jammed probability. During our experiments, we assume that the LLR test knows the information perfectly; i.e., we set exactly the same jamming probability in the LLR test as that used by the jammer. Thus, we refer to this detector as the ideal LLR test. Given the raw data transmission rate of 920 Hz, we set $N =$ 50, 100 and 150 samples such that the corresponding decision time for detection is 54 ms, 109 ms and 163 ms, respectively.

2.5.2.1 Reactive Jamming

We first consider the detection performance of JADE on reactive jamming. Figure 2.13 shows the jamming detection ratios (i.e. the probability that a detector issues an alarm when there indeed exists jamming) of both JADE and the ideal LLR test. We can see that the ideal LLR test outperforms JADE significantly when the jamming probability $p < 0.3$. This is because JADE does not target jamming attacks with jamming probability $p < p^* = 0.3$. Since the phase transition phenomenon has shown that less aggressive jammers cannot dramatically affect the performance of time-critical traffic, a jammer with jamming probability $p < 0.3$ that attempts to evade the JADE detection will fail to cause noticeable message invalidation ratios. It is further observed from Fig. 2.13 that when the jamming probability is greater than 0.3, the ideal LLR test and JADE achieve comparable performance especially when the number of samples N is large. For example, when $N = 150$ and

Table 2.2 Detection ratios of both JADE and likelihood ratio test in the presence of a time-varying jammer

Number of samples	50	100	150	200
JADE	98.6 %	99.1 %	100 %	100 %
LLR test	91.3 %	92.1 %	92.5 %	91.6 %

$p = 0.4$, the detection ratios of JADE and the ideal LLR test are 98.4 % and 99.1 %, respectively. Thus, JADE is able to detect harmful jamming attacks with nearly optimal performance.

It is well known that the performance of the LLR test could be degraded by model mismatch due to imperfect estimation or insufficient profiling. To compare the robustness of JADE with that of the LLR test, we design a sophisticated jammer that keeps changing its jamming probability randomly and uniformly within $[0.4, 0.9]$. In this case, the LLR test first estimates the jamming probability and then performs jamming detection based on the estimation output. Table 2.2 shows the detection ratios of both JADE and the LLR test for $N = 50$, 100, 150, and 200. We can see that JADE is more robust than the LLR test to detect such a time-varying jammer. Because of the model mismatch problem, we observe from Table 2.2 that increasing the number of samples cannot improve the performance of the LLR test.

2.5.2.2 Non-reactive Jamming

We then consider the detection performance of JADE on non-reactive jamming. We use the same network setups as in previous experiments for reactive jamming. The threshold of JADE is set to be $p^* = 0.3$. Figure 2.14 shows the detection performance of JADE on a periodic jammer for different numbers of data samples. We observe that JADE detection performance exhibits a sharp phase transition when the jamming interval I goes from 0.6 to 0.7 ms, indicating that JADE yields very accurate detection for aggressive periodic jammers (small jamming intervals) yet has very poor performance for mild periodic jammers. Although such mild jammers are likely to evade the detection of JADE, it cannot cause severe performance degradation of time-critical applications. Thus, JADE is able to provide accurate detection for both reactive and non-reactive jamming attacks that can cause significant impacts on wireless time-critical applications.

2.5.3 Discussions

Our experimental results showed that JADE achieves efficient and robust jamming detection for aggressive and harmful jammers, at the cost of low detection ratio for less-aggressive jammers. We note that JADE is an application-oriented detector that

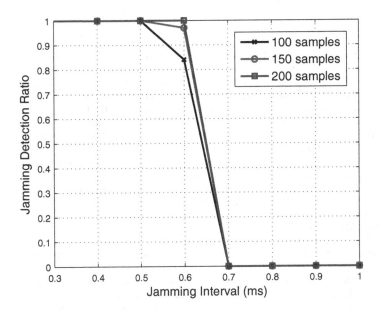

Fig. 2.14 Jamming detection ratios of both JADE and the likelihood ratio test in the presence of a jammer with different jamming probabilities

can be applied directly to practical wireless power systems. It is worthy of noting that during our experiments, we also used the false alarm probability to evaluate the performance of both JADE and the LLR test. We found that neither JADE nor the LLR test issues a jamming alarm when there exists no jamming, since the wireless network is unsaturated and transmission failure rarely happens.

2.6 Summary

In this chapter, we provided an in-depth study on the impact of jamming attacks against time-critical smart grid applications by theoretical modeling and system experiments. We introduced a performance metric, message invalidation ratio, to quantify the impact of jamming attacks. We showed via both analytical analysis and real-time experiments that there exists phase transition phenomena in time-critical applications under a variety of jamming attacks. Based on our analysis and experiments, we designed and implemented the JADE system to achieve efficient and robust jamming detection for power networks. We note that a jamming detection system is only the first step towards providing countermeasures against jamming attacks. In the next chapter, we will design countermeasures to defend against jamming attacks in time-critical wireless networks with applications to the smart grid.

References

1. Aad I, Hubaux JP, Knightly E (2008) Impact of denial of service attacks on ad hoc networks. IEEE/ACM Trans Netw 16:791–802
2. Akyol B, Kirkham H, Clements S, Hadley M (2010) A survey of wireless communications for the electric power system. Technical Report, Pacific Northwest National Laboratory
3. Bayraktaroglu E, King C, Liu X, Noubir G, Rajaraman R, Thapa B (2008) On the performance of IEEE 802.11 under jamming. In: Proceedings of IEEE INFOCOM '08, pp 1265–1273
4. Chiang JT, Hu YC (2008) Dynamic jamming mitigation for wireless broadcast networks. In: Proceedings of IEEE INFOCOM '08
5. Cleveland F (2007) Uses of wireless communications to enhance power system reliability. In: Proceedings of the IEEE Power & Energy Society General Meeting (PES '07)
6. David W (1991) Probability with martingales. Cambridge University Press, Cambridge
7. Emrich S (2007) Dispelling the myths associated with spread spectrum radio technology in electric power SCADA networks. In: Proceedings of the IEEE Power & Energy Society General Meeting (PES '07)
8. GNURadio (2015). http://gnuradio.org/
9. Hamieh A, Ben-Othman J (2009) Detection of jamming attacks in wireless ad hoc networks using error distribution. In: Proceedings of IEEE ICC '09
10. IEC Standard (2003) IEC 61850: communication networks and systems in substations
11. Kanabar PM, Kanabar MG, El-Khattam W, Sidhu TS, Shami A (2009) Evaluation of communication technologies for IEC 61850 based distribution automation system with distributed energy resources. In: Proceedings of the IEEE Power & Energy Society General Meeting (PES '09)
12. Li M, Koutsopoulos I, Poovendran R (2007) Optimal jamming attacks and network defense policies in wireless sensor networks. In: Proceedings of IEEE INFOCOM'07, pp 1307–1315
13. Liu Y, Ning P, Dai H, Liu A (2010) Randomized differential DSSS: jamming-resistant wireless broadcast communication. In: Proceedings of IEEE INFOCOM '10
14. Lu X, Lu Z, Wang W, Ma J (2011) On network performance evaluation toward the smart grid: a case study of DNP3 over TCP/IP. In: Proceedings of IEEE global communications conference (Globecom' 11)
15. Madwifi (2009). http://madwifi.org
16. Malone D, Duffy K, Leith D (2007) Modeling the 802.11 distributed coordination function in nonsaturated heterogeneous conditions. IEEE/ACM Trans Netw 15:159–172
17. Navda V, Bohra A, Ganguly S, Rubenstein D (2007) Using channel hopping to increase 802.11 resilience to jamming attacks. In: Proceedings of IEEE INFOCOM '07, pp 2526–2530
18. NIST News Release (2011) Smart grid panel agrees on standards and guidelines for wireless communication, meter upgrades
19. Office of the National Coordinator for Smart Grid Interoperability (2009) NIST framework and roadmap for smart grid interoperability standards, release 1.0. NIST Special Publication 1108
20. Popper C, Strasser M, Capkun S (2009) Jamming-resistant broadcast communication without shared keys. In: Proceedings of USENIX security symposium (Security '09)
21. Sang L, Arora A (2009) Capabilities of low-power wireless jammers. In: Proceedings of IEEE INFOCOM '09 mini-conference
22. Sidhu TS, Yin Y (2007) Modelling and simulation for performance evaluation of IEC 61850-based substation communication systems. IEEE Trans Power Deliv 22(3):1482–1489
23. Strasser M, Capkun S, Popper C, Cagalj M (2008) Jamming-resistant key establishment using uncoordinated frequency hopping. In: Proceedings of IEEE symposium on security and privacy, pp 64–78
24. Strasser M, Popper C, Capkun S (2009) Efficient uncoordinated FHSS anti-jamming communication. In: Proceedings of MobiHoc '09
25. Toledo AL, Wang X (2008) Robust detection of MAC layer denial-of-service attacks in CSMA/CA wireless networks. IEEE Trans Inf Forensics Secur 3:347–358

26. Wi-Fi Alliance (2009) WiFi for the smart grid: mature, interoperable, security-protected technology for advanced utility management communications
27. Xu W, Trappe W, Zhang Y, Wood T (2005) The feasibility of launching and detecting jamming attacks in wireless networks. In: Proceedings of ACM MobiHoc '05, pp 46–57
28. Zhou HJ, Guo CX, Qin J (2010) Efficient application of GPRS and CDMA networks in SCADA system. In: Proceedings of IEEE power and energy society general meeting (PES '10)

Chapter 3
Minimizing Message Delay of Time-Critical Traffic for Wireless Smart Grid Applications Under Jamming

3.1 Motivation and Related Work

As aforementioned, the smart grid is an emerging cyber-physical system that incorporates networked control mechanisms (e.g, advanced metering and demand response) into conventional power infrastructures [22]. To facilitate information delivery for such mechanisms, wireless networks that provide flexible and untethered network access have been proposed and designed for a variety of smart grid applications [1, 6, 12, 23], such as substation automation [1, 6] and home metering [23]. However, it has been pointed out in [16, 22] that the jamming attack, which uses radio interference to disrupt wireless communications [14, 20, 25], can result in network performance degradation and even denial-of-service in power applications, thereby becoming a primary security threat to prevent the deployment of wireless networks for the smart grid. It is of crucial importance not only to model and detect jamming attacks, but also to defend against such attacks in time-critical wireless applications in the smart grid.

There have been extensive works on designing spread spectrum based communication schemes, which provide jamming resilience to conventional wireless networks by using multiple orthogonal frequency [20, 21] or code [14, 17] channels. Interesting enough, most efforts adopt a case-by-case (or model-by-model) methodology to investigate how a message can be sent to its destination. In other words, based on commonly-adopted jamming attack models (e.g., periodic, memoryless, and reactive models [3]), existing works focus on designing anti-jamming communication schemes for message delivery in conventional wireless networks.

However, the NIST has recently imposed a strong requirement for smart grid security: *power system operations must be able to continue during any security attack or compromise (as much as possible)* [22]. This means that the widely-used case-by-case methodology cannot be readily adapted to wireless smart grid

© The Author(s) 2015
Z. Lu et al., *Modeling and Evaluating Denial of Service Attacks for Wireless and Mobile Applications*, SpringerBriefs in Computer Science,
DOI 10.1007/978-3-319-23288-1_3

applications, because it is not able to guarantee reliable communication under any potential jamming attack. To provide such a guarantee, securing wireless smart grid applications requires a paradigm shift from the case-by-case methodology to a new *worst-case* methodology that offers performance assurance under any attack scenario. On the other hand, it has been shown that the message delay performance can be substantially worsen and even violate the timing requirement of control applications under inappropriate security design. For example, in an experimental substation network [15], if a RSA-based scheme is used for authenticating *trip protection* messages, 40 % messages cannot be delivered and verified under the timing requirement of 3 ms. This show that in addition to the necessity of using the worst-case methodology, security design for the smart grid should also attempt to minimize the message delay such that it always meets the timing requirement. As a result, in this chapter, we aim at solving a fundamental yet open question for wireless smart grid applications: *how to minimize the message delay under worst-case jamming attacks*. The answer to this question can not only help us design network strategies against worst-case jamming attacks in wireless smart grid applications, but also offer general guidance into jamming defense strategies in cyber-physical systems.

In this chapter, we address this issue by considering a wireless network that uses multiple frequency and code channels to provide jamming resilience for smart grid applications. We consider two general jamming-resilient communication modes for smart grid applications: coordinated and uncoordinated modes [14, 20, 21]. In coordinated mode, the sender and receiver share a common secret or key (e.g., code-frequency channel assignment), which is unknown to attackers. Accordingly, an attacker has to choose its own strategy to disrupt the communication between the transmitter and receiver. Coordinated communication is a conventional model in spread spectrum systems. However, the transmitter and receiver may not share a common secret initially (e.g., a node joins a network and attempts to establish a secret with others). Uncoordinated communication is therefore used to help establish such an initial key. In uncoordinated communication, the sender and receiver randomly choose a frequency-code channel to transmit and receive, respectively. A message can be delivered from the sender to the receiver only if they both reside at the same channel, and at the same time the jammer does not disrupt the transmission on the channel.

As power applications are time-critical with strict timing requirements (e.g. 3 ms and 10 ms in substation trip protection [11]), message delivery becomes invalid as long as its delay D is greater than the delay threshold σ. Therefore, different from existing metrics (e.g. throughput or packet delivery ratio [25]) to evaluate the jamming impact in conventional wireless networks, we use the message invalidation probability $\mathbb{P}(D > \sigma)$, which directly reflects timing requirements of power applications, to measure the jamming impact in the smart grid. Our goal is to minimize $\mathbb{P}(D > \sigma)$ under the worst-case jamming attack. To this end, we first define a generic jamming process that includes a wide range of existing jamming models. Then, we show via theoretical analysis that in all strategies under the generic process, the worst-case message delay $\mathbb{P}(D > \sigma)$ is a U-shaped[1] function of the network traffic load. This indicates that, interestingly, increasing a fair amount of traffic into the network can improve the delay performance for wireless smart grid applications under the worst-case attack.

Accordingly, we propose a very lightweight yet promising method, TACT (transmitting adaptive camouflage traffic). TACT adaptively generates redundant traffic called *camouflage traffic* into the network such that the overall network traffic load is balanced at the optimal point to minimize the worst-case message delay. We implement TACT in our micro smart grid, Green Hub [2], to defend wireless power applications against jamming attacks. Our contributions are threefold.

1. Towards existing works on jamming attacks, we present a paradigm shift from the case-by-case methodology to the worst-case methodology that offers a new and important design method for performance assurance in wireless smart grid applications.
2. By defining a generic jamming process, we find via theoretical analysis that the worst-case message delay is a U-shaped function of network traffic load. We show that there exists a unique traffic load to minimize the worst-case message delay in the smart grid. Our results indicate that transmitting camouflage traffic is an effective way to combat the worst-case attack.
3. Based on theoretical analysis, we design the TACT system to minimize the message delay in the smart grid under jamming. Experiments show that TACT can decrease the message invalidation probability in order of magnitude for smart grid applications.

To the best of our knowledge, this work is the first work that reports such an interesting U-shaped delay property for wireless applications under jamming attacks, and TACT is the first experimental system that combats jamming attacks for smart grid applications.

The rest of this chapter is organized as follows. In Sect. 3.2, we introduce preliminaries and models. In Sects. 3.3–3.5, we derive the theoretical results, design the method of TACT, then implement TACT in Green Hub, respectively. Finally, we conclude in Sect. 3.6.

3.2 Preliminaries and Problem Formulation

In this section, we first introduce backgrounds on wireless networks for the smart grid, then present network and jamming models, finally formulate the research problem.

---

[1]Mathematically, a function is said to be U-shaped if it is first-decreasing, then-increasing.

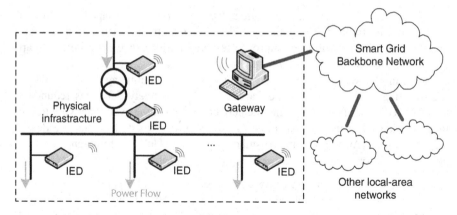

Fig. 3.1 A wireless local-area network in the smart grid

3.2.1 Backgrounds on Wireless Networks for the Smart Grid

Wireless networks in the smart grid are in general used for local-area smart grid applications, such as substation automation and distributed energy management [6, 12]. As shown in Fig. 3.1, the wireless network for a local-area power system consists of a number of intelligent electronic devices (IEDs) and the gateway node. IEDs are devices installed on physical infrastructures to fulfill power management procedures by communicating with each other. The gateway is connected to the smart grid backbone network. Local-area messages can be forwarded via the gateway to outside networks.

Due to the broadcast nature of wireless channels, wireless networks for the smart grid are inevitably exposed to jamming attacks, which transmit radio interference to prevent legitimate messages from being received [14, 20, 25]. It has already been pointed out that jamming attacks, by disrupting communication between power equipments, can possibly result in grid operation instability or even regional blackout [13]. Therefore, wireless networks for the smart grid must have the ability to combat jamming attacks. There are two widely-used spread spectrum techniques [4, 14, 17, 20] to defend against jamming attacks in the literature.

- Frequency hopping spread spectrum (FHSS): the sender and receiver switch a frequency channel among a pool of candidate channels from time to time. The jammer can only jam a transmission when it is on the same channel.
- Direct sequence spread spectrum (DSSS): the sender multiplies the original data with a pseudo-noise (PN) sequence (called a code channel). The receiver uses a correlator with the same PN sequence to recover the original message. It is difficult for a jammer to disrupt the communication over the code channel unless it knows the PN sequence used by the channel.

Both FHSS and DSSS have been proposed and used for power applications [5, 8, 12, 13]. For example, a DSSS based system is demonstrated in [5] for local substation automation. Since FHSS and DSSS provide jamming resilience by using multiple orthogonal frequency and code channels, a trivial solution for decreasing the message delay is to increase the number of frequency or code channels. Then, a jammer will have a lower chance to transmit jamming signals on the same channel used by a transmit-receive pair. However, it is quite undesirable in practice because of the large cost of network spectrum resources. Therefore, we attempt to minimize the message delay in a wireless network with fixed numbers of frequency and code channels.

3.2.2 Network Model

We consider a wireless local-area network $\mathcal{N}(m, N_f, N_c)$, where m is the number of nodes (including IEDs and the gateway) in the network, N_f and N_c are the numbers of frequency and code channels, respectively. There are two major types of traffic flows in the network.

1. Local traffic, which is generated from one node to another for local monitoring or protection.
2. Outside traffic, which is between a node and an outside node via the smart grid backbone network.

For a message going outside, it will be delivered first from an IED to the gateway via the local-area wireless network (local delivery), then to the destination network via the smart grid backbone network. If there exists a jammer in the network, it can affect the delay performance of both local and outside traffic types. For outside traffic, the delay component for the first local delivery can dominate in the overall end-to-end delay, since the smart grid backbone network is always of high bandwidth. Therefore, we focus on the message delay of local traffic in the network.

It is worth noting that in the smart grid, a large amount of network traffic features a constant traffic model for continuous monitoring and control of power equipments [11, 12, 19]. In addition, nodes can have distinct network traffic loads for different applications. For example, merging-unit IEDs in a substation can send data of sampled power signal quality at various rates of 960–4800 messages/s, dependent on configuration [19]. Thus, we assume that there are heterogeneous traffic loads in network $\mathcal{N}(m, N_f, N_c)$; i.e., node i has a constant traffic load of λ_i messages/s $(i \in \{1, 2, \cdots, m\})$ in the network.

3.2.3 Communication and Interference Models

3.2.3.1 Protocol Processing

In the smart grid, to ensure in-time monitoring and control of power devices, a large amount of communication messages have stringent timing requirements. For example, substation applications have 3–500 ms delay constraints for message delivery [11]. We refer to such messages as *time-critical* messages. The nature of time-critical messages indicates that they should be immediately transmitted and avoid being buffered. For example, time-critical messaging in substation communications [11] features a simple transmission mechanism at the application layer: bypass TCP and retransmit the same message multiple times to ensure timely delivery and reliability. Thus, we also adopt such a mechanism at the application layer of each node.

When a message is passed from the application layer to the MAC layer, traditionally, CSMA/CA is used to sense the channel activity before sending the message. However, CSMA/CA is primarily designed for one-channel networks, and may not be efficient in spread spectrum systems. In network $\mathcal{N}(m, N_f, N_c)$, the wireless channel is separated into N_f frequency and N_c code channels. Such channels can be considered orthogonal to each other [10]. Even if there are multiple wireless transmissions over the same frequency channel, they will be successfully decoded at receivers as long as they use distinct code channels. CSMA/CA, which defers a transmission after sensing any activity on a frequency channel, may unintentionally degrade the delay performance.

Thus, we assume that when the MAC layer receives a message from upper layers, it will directly transmit the message on a frequency-code channel pair, denoted as the (i,j)th channel shown in Fig. 3.2. Since the application layer will retransmit the message multiple times, the MAC layer will assign a distinct frequency-code channel to each retransmission.

In order to successfully receive the message, the receiver must reside on the same frequency-code channel used by the sender. However, the receiver may or may not have the information of the sender's channel assignment, which leads to distinct

Fig. 3.2 Available channels: N_f frequency channels and N_c code channels

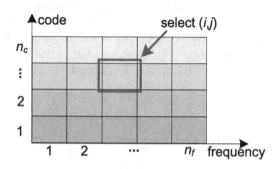

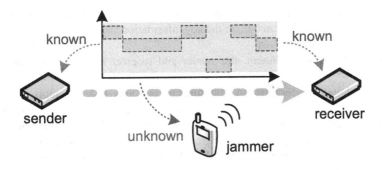

Fig. 3.3 Coordinated communication: the sender and the receiver share the common secret channel assignment, which is unknown to others

communication modes between the sender and receiver. In what follows, we will introduce and consider extensively-used models in anti-jamming communications.

3.2.3.2 Secret Communications and Key Establishment

As mentioned previously, two communicators may or may not share a common secret channel assignment (the key) with each other. If they do share a key, it can be assumed that the receiver can perfectly synchronize with the sender's frequency-code channel switching, which is called *coordinated communication mode*. In this mode, we assume that for a sender-receiver pair, each channel assignment is uniformly distributed over all $N_f N_c$ channel selections such that the chance of potential channel collision among legitimate nodes can be minimized.

Coordinated communication happens only when two communicators share a common secret unknown to others, as shown in Fig. 3.3. However, they initially may not have such a secret. In fact, it is commonly adopted in the literature (e.g., [17, 20, 21]) that they share no secret key before they attempt to communicate with each other. Then, how to establish the key before they can use the key to communicate coordinatedly? To solve the question, a wide-adopted solution in the literature (e.g., [17, 20, 21]) is *uncoordinated communication mode*, which is shown as follows.

First, assume that the two communicators can always verify each other's authenticity. For example, their public keys are open to everyone. Every packet transmitted by the sender is digitally signed by the sender's private key. Then, after successfully receiving a packet from the wireless channel, the receiver can use the sender's public key to verify if the packet is indeed sent by the real sender.

Second, in order to establish the key, the sender keeps sending the key information to a randomly selected frequency/code channel. The information can be encrypted such that it is only decodable to the real receiver, e.g., using the receiver's public key to encrypt. At the same time, the receiver randomly chooses a frequency/code channel to listen on. When the sender and receiver reside on the same channel, the sender can deliver the key information successfully to the receiver to finish the key establishment.

After the key establishment, the sender and receiver have shared a common secret key, so they can use the key to communicate with each other. We can see that although uncoordinated communication looks less efficient, it is still essential to achieve coordinated communication. As a result, both uncoordinated and coordinated modes are vital for securing jamming-resilient communications.

Since channel selection is random in the uncoordinated mode, we adopt the uniform selection strategy [18], in which both sender and receiver uniformly choose channels to transmit and receive, respectively.

3.2.3.3   Interference Model

In coordinated communication, the sender and receiver have the common knowledge of the secret channel assignment, and can synchronize with each other. The transmission on a channel fails only when it is disrupted by jamming or other transmissions at the same channel. Thus, we assume that for coordinated communication, the message delivery on the (i,j)th channel fails when at least one of the following two events holds.

1. At least a portion ρ ($0 < \rho < 1$) of the transmission is disrupted by jamming on the (i,j)th channel;
2. At least a portion ρ of the transmission collides with other legitimate traffic on the (i,j)th channel;

For uncoordinated communication, the failure of a message delivery can be caused by not only jamming or other transmissions on the same channel, but also the channel selection mismatch between the sender and receiver. Therefore, we assume that the message delivery with duration T_L on the (i,j)th channel fails if at least one of the following holds.

1. At least a portion ρ of the transmission is disrupted by jamming on the (i,j)th channel;
2. At least a portion ρ of the transmission collides with other legitimate traffic on the (i,j)th channel;
3. During the message transmission, the receiver resides on the (i,j)th channel for a time duration smaller than $(1-\rho)T_L$.

Note that the exact value of ρ varies in practice, depending on error correction coding schemes. For example, the standard (255,223) Reed-Solomon code is used in the transmission, it is capable of correcting up to 16 bit errors among every 223 information bits [14], resulting in $\rho \approx 7.1\%$.

3.2.4 Generic Jamming Model

The objective of a jammer is to broadcast radio interference to disrupt messages as many as possible in network $\mathcal{N}(m, N_f, N_c)$. As the network has multiple channels, the jammer can adopt a wide range of strategies to disrupt message delivery. In the literature, there are two major jamming types in terms of jamming behavior: non-reactive and reactive models [14, 17, 20, 21, 25]. Non-reactive jammers transmit radio interference by following their own strategies. Reactive jammers transmit interference only when they sense any activity on a wireless channel. In addition, a jammer can either target a single frequency-code channel or have the ability to attack multiple channels at the same time. In this work, we assume that the jammer has the knowledge of the pool of candidate channels used in the network, and attempt to choose the best strategy to attack one or some of the channels and lead the worst-case attack. In order to adopt varying strategies the jammer can use, we define a generic process to accommodate various jamming behaviors and models in the literature.

Definition 3.1 (Generic Jamming Process). A jammer's jamming process is denoted as a Markov-renewal process

$$((\mathbf{F}, \mathbf{C}), X) = \{(\mathbf{F}_k, \mathbf{C}_k), X_k | k = 1, 2, \cdots\},$$

where X_k is the renewal interval representing the jamming duration at the kth state, denoted by $(\mathbf{F}_k, \mathbf{C}_k) = \{(F_{k,i}, C_{k,i})\}_{i \in [1,s]}$, the set of frequency and code channels targeted by the jammer, $(F_{k,i}, C_{k,i})$ is a particular frequency and code channel, and s is the number of channels the jammer can attack simultaneously. The embedded transition matrices associated with states $(\mathbf{F}_k, \mathbf{C}_k)$ are denoted as $\mathbf{Q}_f$ and $\mathbf{Q}_c$, respectively. When the jamming is non-reactive, $((\mathbf{F}, \mathbf{C}), X)$ is assumed to be a continuous Markov process. When the jamming is reactive, $X_k = \tau + S_k \mathbf{1}_A,$[2] where τ is the constant channel sensing time, S_k is the duration of the jamming signal, A denotes the event that at least one channel in set $(\mathbf{F}_k, \mathbf{C}_k)$ is sensed busy.

Remark 3.1. The generic jamming process can characterize both non-reactive and reactive jammers that change jamming status over time. In addition, it also models jammers that can attack $s \geq 1$ frequency-code channels at the same time. Thus, the generic model defined in Definition 3.1 can represent a wide range of existing jamming models and strategies in the literature. For example, consider a simple network with four frequency channels in the presence of a jammer that can attack only one frequency channel at the same time. If the jammer's transition matrix $\mathbf{Q}_f$ is the 4×4 identity matrix with state transitions shown in Fig. 3.4, every state is

---

[2] $\mathbf{1}_A$ denotes the indicator function, which has the value 1 for A and the value 0 for A^c.

Fig. 3.4 Constant jamming

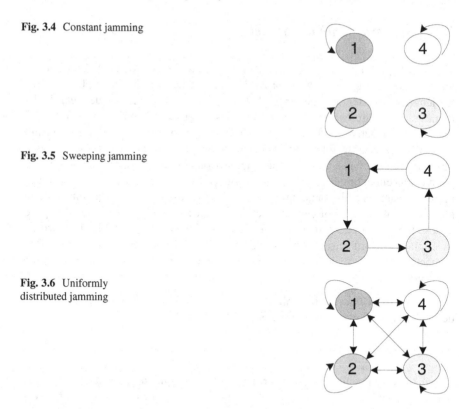

Fig. 3.5 Sweeping jamming

Fig. 3.6 Uniformly
distributed jamming

an absorbing state and the process represents continuous jamming on a particular
channel [25]. Similarly, Figs. 3.5 and 3.6 represent sweeping jamming [9] and
uniformly-distributed jamming, respectively.

As we can see in the Markov-renewal model, $\{X_k\}$ and $\{(\mathbf{F}_k, \mathbf{C}_k)\}$ can directly
reflect when a certain set of channels is affected by the jamming attack, and matrices
$\mathbf{Q}_f$ and $\mathbf{Q}_c$ can model what the jamming strategy is.

3.2.5 Problem Formulation

The primary goal of smart grid communication is to achieve timely monitoring
and control for power control applications. Therefore, the delay performance is of
critical importance in the smart grid. A time-critical message becomes invalid as
long as its message delay D is greater than its delay constraint σ. As a result, we
focus on how to minimize the message invalidation probability $\mathbb{P}(D > \sigma)$ in network
$\mathcal{N}(m, N_f, N_c)$ under the generic jamming process $((\mathbf{F}, \mathbf{C}), X)$.

It is worth noting that there are two opposites in the network: the network operator always attempts to minimize the message delay; in contrast, the jammer always

intends to maximize the message delay. The lowest bound of the message delay is always achieved when there exists no jammer or a naive jammer. As the NIST requires smart grid operations must continue under any potential attack, we adopt a worst-case methodology to study the problem of minimizing message delay in the smart grid under jamming attacks.

1. In wireless local-area network $\mathcal{N}(m, N_f, N_c)$, for a time-critical application with delay threshold σ, what is the worst-case delay performance $\mathbb{P}(D > \sigma)$ under the generic jamming process $((\mathbf{F}, \mathbf{C}), X)$.
2. Given the worst-case scenario in Step 1, how to minimize $\mathbb{P}(D > \sigma)$.

In the next section, we use theoretical analysis to show the worst-case delay performance under jamming attacks.

3.3 Theoretical Analysis

In this section, we theoretically analyze the worst-case delay performance for wireless smart grid applications under the generic jamming model. We first consider the worst case in coordinated communication, then the worst case in uncoordinated communication. Finally, we propose a method to minimize the worst-case delay for both coordinated and uncoordinated modes.

3.3.1 Jamming Impact on Coordinated Communications

Our goal is to find the jamming attack that maximizes $\mathbb{P}(D > \sigma)$ in the network such that we can identify the worst-case attack targeting wireless smart grid applications. As our generic jamming process characterizes both non-reactive and reactive jammers with distinct behaviors, we provide analytical results of their impacts on $\mathbb{P}(D > \sigma)$, respectively.

Lemma 3.1 (Non-reactive Jamming). *In wireless local-area network $\mathcal{N}(m, N_f, N_c)$ in the presence of a non-reactive jamming process $\{(\mathbf{F}, \mathbf{C}), X\}$ with ability to attack s channels simultaneously, the message delay D_k of a time-critical application at node k satisfies*

$$\mathbb{P}(D_k > \sigma) \leq \left(1 - \left(1 - \frac{1}{N_f N_c}\right)^{T_L(1-\rho)\gamma_k} \left(1 - \frac{(1-\rho)s}{\rho N_f N_c}\right)\right)^{\sigma/T_L}, \qquad (3.1)$$

where T_L is the message transmission duration, σ is the message delay threshold, $\gamma_k = \sum_{j=1, j \neq k}^{m} \lambda_j$, and λ_j is the traffic rate at node j.

Proof. Without loss of generality, assume that node 1 is transmitting a message with delay threshold σ. Each transmission has a duration of T_L. The application layer can transmit the message at most $\lfloor \sigma/T_L \rfloor$ times (for the sake of simplicity, we in the following assume that σ/T_L is an integer, i.e., $\lfloor \sigma/T_L \rfloor = \sigma/T_L$, which does not affect the derivation of our main results). Among all σ/T_L transmission attempts, the ith one uses the (u_i, v_i)th channel ($1 \leq i \leq \sigma/T_L$).

The message invalidation probability $\mathbb{P}(D_1 > \sigma)$ is equal to the probability that all σ/T_L transmission attempts are disrupted by either collision or jamming, i.e.,

$$\mathbb{P}(D_1 > \sigma) = \mathbb{P}\left(\cap_{i=1}^{\sigma/T_L} (J_i \cup C_i) \right), \tag{3.2}$$

where C_i and J_i denote the events that the ith transmission is disrupted by collision and jamming, respectively.

First, we derive the collision probability $\mathbb{P}(C_i)$. Suppose that node 1's ith transmission starts at time 0, a collision that can successfully disrupt node 1's transmission will happen if another node makes a transmission attempt during period $[0, (1-\rho)T_L]$ and at the same time uses the same channel. Since all nodes have constant traffic rates, there are $(1-\rho)T_L \sum_{j=2}^m \lambda_j$ transmissions at other nodes that can possibly disrupt node 1's transmission. As the frequency-code channel for each transmission in the network is uniformly assigned among all $N_f N_c$ selections, the collision probability is equal to the probability that there is at least one other transmission colliding with node 1's ith transmission, which can be written as

$$\mathbb{P}(C_i) = 1 - (1 - 1/(N_f N_c))^{(1-\rho)T_L \gamma_1}, \tag{3.3}$$

where $\gamma_1 = \sum_{j=2}^m \lambda_j$.

Then, we compute the jamming probability $\mathbb{P}(J_i)$. The jamming process $\{(\mathbf{F}, \mathbf{C}), X\}$ has renewal intervals $\{X_l\}$. Let N_i represent how many times the jammer makes a state transition, and we have

$$N_i = \sup_{n \in \mathbb{N}} \left\{ \sum_{l=1}^n X_l < (1-\rho)T_L \right\}, \quad \mathbb{N} = \{0, 1, 2, \cdots\}$$

where $X_1, \cdots, X_{N_i}$ are jamming intervals during the ith transmission. In order to successfully disrupt the ith transmission (i.e., J_i holds), the sum of jamming intervals on the (i, j)th channel must be larger than the threshold ρT_L. Letting B_l be the event that the lth interval with length X_l hits the (u_i, v_i)'th channel (i.e., $B_l = \{u_i \in F_l, v_i \in C_l\}$), we obtain

$$\mathbb{P}(J_i | u_i, v_i) = \mathbb{P}\left(\sum_{l=1}^{N_i} X_l \mathbf{1}_{B_l} \geq \rho T_L \right) \leq \frac{\mathbb{E}\left(\sum_{l=1}^{N_i} X_l \mathbf{1}_{B_l} \right)}{\rho T_L}$$

$$= \mathbb{E}(N_i)\mathbb{E}(X_l)\mathbb{P}(B_l)/(\rho T_L), \tag{3.4}$$

where the last equality and inequality follows from Wald's equation and Markov's inequality respectively, $\mathbb{E}(N_i) = (1-\rho)T_L/\mathbb{E}(X_l)$ and $\mathbb{P}(B_l)$ denotes the probability that the jamming hits the (u_i, v_i)th channel. Since (u_i, v_i) is uniformly assigned, it follows from (3.4) that

$$\mathbb{P}(J_i) \leq \sum_{p=1}^{N_f} \sum_{q=1}^{N_c} \mathbb{E}(N_i)\mathbb{E}(X_l)\mathbb{P}(B_l)/(\rho T_L)/(N_f N_c)$$

$$\leq \frac{(1-\rho)T_L}{\mathbb{E}(X_l)}\mathbb{E}(X_l)\frac{s}{N_f N_c}\frac{1}{\rho T_L} = \frac{(1-\rho)s}{\rho N_f N_c}. \tag{3.5}$$

Finally, combining (3.2), (3.3) and (3.5) finishes the proof. □

Next, we present our theoretical results on reactive jamming.

Lemma 3.2 (Reactive Jamming). *In wireless local-area network $\mathcal{N}(m, N_f, N_c)$ in the presence of a reactive jammer $\{(\mathbf{F}, \mathbf{C}), X\}$ that has sensing time τ and can attack s channels simultaneously, for a time-critical application at node k, its message delivery delay D_k satisfies*

$$\mathbb{P}(D_k > \sigma) \leq \left(1 - \left(1 - \frac{1}{N_f N_c}\right)^{T_L(1-\rho)\gamma_k}\left(1 - \frac{sT_L}{\frac{\tau N_f N_c}{1-\rho} + \rho T_L^2 \gamma_k}\right)\right)^{\sigma/T_L}, \tag{3.6}$$

where T_L is the message transmission duration, σ is the message delay threshold, $\gamma_k = \sum_{j=1, j \neq k}^{m} \lambda_j$, and λ_j is the traffic rate at node j.

Proof. Similar to the proof for Lemma 3.1, assume that node 1 is transmitting a message with delay threshold σ. The transmission resides at the (u_i, v_i)th channel for the ith attempt. To find $\mathbb{P}(D_1 > \sigma)$, we first need to compute both collision and jamming probabilities, $\mathbb{P}(C_i)$ and $\mathbb{P}(J_i)$. As $\mathbb{P}(C_i)$ is given in (3.3), we in the following compute $\mathbb{P}(J_i)$.

For the sake of simplicity, assume that the ith transmission starts at time 0. Define a renewal process $N_i(t)$ as

$$N_i(t) = \sup_{n \in \mathbb{N}}\left\{\sum_{l=1}^{n} X_l < t\right\}, \quad \mathbb{N} = \{0, 1, 2, \cdots\}. \tag{3.7}$$

Then $X_1, X_2, \cdots, X_{N_i(t)}$ are renewal intervals during period $[0, t]$. Different from non-reactive jamming, reactive jamming has renewal intervals $X_l = \tau + S_l \mathbf{1}_A$, where A denotes the event that a channel is sensed with activity, and S_l is the jamming duration. To maximize its damage to the network, the reactive jammer should always set the jamming duration S_l to be ρT_L. This means that when the jammer senses a transmission, it always chooses the minimum effective jamming duration to disrupt the transmission such that it can immediately move on to sense and jam other channels. Thus, we choose $S_l = \rho T_L$.

In order to successfully disrupt the ith transmission (e.g., J_i holds), the reactive jammer must switch to the (u_i, v_i)th channel at least once during $[0, (1-\rho)T_L - \tau]$. Let event $B_l = \{u_i \in \mathbf{F}_l | v_i \in \mathbf{C}_l\}$. Then, $\mathbb{P}(J_i | u_i, v_i) = \mathbb{P}\left(\sum_{l=1}^{N_i((1-\rho)T_L-\tau)} \mathbf{1}_{B_l} \geq 1\right)$. Using similar procedures in (3.4) and (3.5), we have

$$\mathbb{P}(J_i) \leq \mathbb{E}(N_i((1-\rho)T_L - \tau)s/(N_f N_c). \tag{3.8}$$

To obtain $\mathbb{E}(N_i((1-\rho)T_L - \tau)$, we first have from the elementary renewal theorem

$$\lim_{t \to \infty} \mathbb{E}(N_i(t))/t = 1/\mathbb{E}(X_l), \tag{3.9}$$

where $\mathbb{E}(X_l) = \tau + \rho T_L \mathbb{P}(A)$, $\mathbb{P}(A)$ is the probability that a channel is sensed busy and $\mathbb{P}(A) = 1 - (1 - 1/(N_f N_c))^{(1-\rho)T_L \gamma_l}$. Then, it is reasonable to assume that the sensing time $\tau \ll T_L$ and the average renewal interval $\mathbb{E}(X_l) \ll T_L$ since power networks should always have unsaturated traffic loads [11, 12] for timely monitoring and control. Thus, from (3.9), $\mathbb{E}(N_i((1-\rho)T_L - \tau)$ can be approximated as

$$\mathbb{E}(N_i((1-\rho)T_L - \tau)) \approx \frac{(1-\rho)T_L - \tau}{\mathbb{E}(X_l)} \approx \frac{(1-\rho)T_L}{\mathbb{E}(X_l)}$$

$$= \frac{(1-\rho)T_L}{\tau + \rho T_L - \rho T_L \left(1 - \frac{1}{N_f N_c}\right)^{(1-\rho)T_L \gamma_l}} \approx \frac{(1-\rho)T_L}{\tau + \frac{\rho(1-\rho)T_L \gamma_l}{N_f N_c}}. \tag{3.10}$$

The last approximation follows from the fact that $(1-x)^a \approx 1 - ax$ for small x. From (3.8) and (3.10), we obtain

$$\mathbb{P}(J_i) \leq \frac{(1-\rho)s T_L}{\tau N_f N_c + \rho(1-\rho)T_L^2 \gamma_l}. \tag{3.11}$$

Combining (3.2), (3.3) and (3.11) completes the proof. $\qquad\square$

Based on Lemmas 3.1 and 3.2, we show in the following that reactive jamming in general leads to the worst-case delay performance, thereby maximizing the damage to the network.

Theorem 3.1 (Worst-Case Delay in Coordinated Mode). *For wireless local-area network* $\mathscr{N}(m, N_f, N_c)$ *under coordinated communication, the worst-case delay performance at node k is induced by reactive jamming with sensing time τ sufficiently small. Specifically, the message delay D_k satisfies*

$$\mathbb{P}(D_k > \sigma) \leq \left(1 - \left(1 - \frac{1}{N_f N_c}\right)^{T_L(1-\rho)\gamma_k} \left(1 - \frac{s T_L}{\frac{\tau N_f N_c}{1-\rho} + \rho T_L^2 \gamma_k}\right)\right)^{\sigma/T_L}, \tag{3.12}$$

where T_L is the message transmission duration, σ is the message delay threshold, $\gamma_k = \sum_{j=1, j \neq k}^{m} \lambda_j$, and λ_j is the traffic rate at node j.

Proof. Comparing with (3.1) and (3.6), it suffices to show

$$\frac{(1-\rho)sT_L}{\tau N_f N_c + \rho(1-\rho)T_L^2 \gamma_k} \geq \frac{(1-\rho)s}{\rho N_f N_c}, \tag{3.13}$$

which is equivalent to

$$\tau \leq \rho T_L - \rho(1-\rho)T_L^2 \gamma_k/(N_f N_c) \tag{3.14}$$

In order for (3.14) to hold for τ sufficiently small, it suffices to show that the right-hand side of (3.14) is larger than 0, i.e., $\rho T_L - \rho(1-\rho)T_L^2 \gamma_k/(N_f N_c) > 0$. Let $\hat{\gamma}$ be the overall message rate in the network and B be the maximum bit rate supported by each sub-channel. Then, a single message includes $T_L B$ bits, and the overall network traffic rate (in terms of bits/second) can be written as $\hat{r} = T_L B \hat{\gamma}$, which is smaller than the overall channel bandwidth $N_f N_c B$. In other words, we have $\hat{r} = T_L B \hat{\gamma} \leq N_f N_c B$, i.e., $T_L \hat{\gamma} \leq N_f N_c$. Since it always holds that $\gamma_k \leq \hat{\gamma}$, we have $T_L \gamma_k \leq N_f N_c$ and

$$\rho T_L - \frac{\rho(1-\rho)T_L^2 \gamma_k}{N_f N_c} \geq \rho T_L - \rho(1-\rho)T_L = \rho^2 T_L > 0, \tag{3.15}$$

which finishes the proof. $\square$

Remark 3.2. Theorem 3.1 shows that reactive jamming with sensing time τ sufficiently small will induce the worst-case performance. Theoretically, we can always assume that τ is arbitrarily small and consider reactive jamming as the worst case. Will reactive jamming do so in practice? The essence of the question is how small τ can be for a practical jammer. Taking a closer look at (3.14), we find that the right-hand side can be approximated as ρT_L when the pool of channel selections is large (i.e., $N_f N_c$ is large), which is true for an effective anti-jamming system. This indicates that reactive jamming is more harmful than non-reactive jamming when τ is smaller than the minimum jamming duration ρT_L. It has been shown that τ can be designed very small, depending on implementation; while ρT_L should be kept relatively large to effectively disrupt a transmission. For example, a software-defined radio based jammer [24] needs 20 μs to sense an 802.15.4 transmission and send jamming signals for at least 26 μs to disrupt the transmission. Such a sensing time can be further shorten with a hardware implementation instead of a software implementation, which demonstrates that τ is indeed smaller than ρT_L in practice. Therefore, it is reasonable to consider reactive jamming as the worst-case scenario in wireless smart grid applications both theoretically and practically.

Figure 3.7 shows an example of the worst-case message invalidation probabilities induced by both non-reactive (3.1) and reactive jamming (3.6) for time-critical applications at node k. We can see that reactive jamming always leads to worse

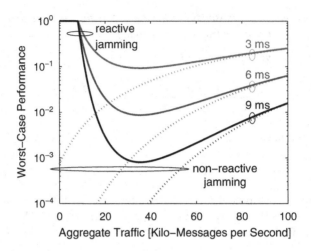

Fig. 3.7 Coordinated communication: worst-case delay performance $\mathbb{P}(D_k > \sigma)$ versus aggregate traffic γ_k at node k for time-critical applications with delay thresholds of 3–9 ms ($N_f = N_c = 10$, $T_L = 1$ ms, $\rho = 0.1$, and $\tau = 100\,\mu$s for reactive jamming)

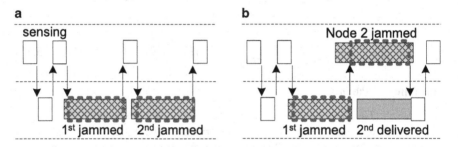

Fig. 3.8 Message delivery without/with other traffic under reactive jamming. (**a**) jamming without other traffic (**b**) jamming with other traffic

delay performance than non-reactive jamming, and that the delay performance at node k also depends on the aggregate traffic load γ_k. An interesting observation from Fig. 3.7 is that in the reactive-jamming case, the message invalidation probability is not minimized at $\gamma_k^* = 0$. Instead, it is minimized at a fairly large value $\gamma_k^* \approx 38$ kilo-messages/s.

Figure 3.7 illustrates that, interestingly, the worst-case delay (caused by reactive jamming) is in fact a U-shaped (first-decreasing then-increasing) function of traffic load γ_k. This is due to the sensing and reacting nature of reactive jamming.

Consider a simple example: Fig. 3.8a shows two transmissions of a message by node 1 with two-channel frequency-hopping. If there is no other traffic, by scanning the two channels alternately, a reactive jammer can always sense and jam both transmissions. If node 2 is also transmitting as shown in Fig. 3.8b, the jammer can also sense and attempt to disrupt node 2's transmission. Then, there is a chance that node 1's message can be delivered during the time that the jammer is jamming node 2's transmission. Thus, fairly increasing network traffic load can in fact improve the delay performance under reactive jamming. On the other hand, the over-increase of traffic will surely decrease the performance since transmissions have a high probability to collide with each other. Hence, there should be an optimal traffic load such that the worst-case message delay can be minimized.

In the following, we show theoretically that there exists a traffic load γ_k^* to minimize the worst-case message invalidation probability for node k in the network.

Theorem 3.2 (Optimal Load in Coordinated Mode). *In wireless network $\mathcal{N}(m, N_f, N_c)$, node k's worse-case message invalidation probability (3.12) in coordinated communication is minimized at*

$$\gamma_k^* = \frac{1}{\rho(1-\rho)T_L^2}\left(\frac{\sqrt{c_2^2 - 4c_1\rho T_L^2} - c_2}{2c_1} - \tau N_f N_c\right),$$

where $c_1 = \ln(1 - 1/(N_f N_c))$ and $c_2 = (1-\rho)T_L$.

Proof. It is equivalent to show that γ_k^* maximizes the following function.

$$f(\gamma_k) = \left(1 - \frac{1}{N_f N_c}\right)^{T_L(1-\rho)\gamma_k}\left(1 - \frac{(1-\rho)T_L}{\tau N_f N_c + \rho(1-\rho)T_L^2\gamma_k}\right). \tag{3.16}$$

Letting $\nabla_{\gamma_k} f(\gamma_k^*) = 0$ results in a quadratic equation

$$c_1 w^2 - c_2 w + \rho T_L^2 = 0, \tag{3.17}$$

where $c_1 = \ln(1 - 1/(N_f N_c))$, $c_2 = (1-\rho)T_L$, and

$$w = \tau N_f N_c + \rho(1-\rho)T_L^2\gamma_k^*. \tag{3.18}$$

Solving Eq. (3.17) for w yields

$$w = (\sqrt{c_2^2 - 4c_1\rho T_L^2} - c_2)/(2c_1). \tag{3.19}$$

Combining (3.18) with (3.19) completes the proof. $\square$

Remark 3.3. Theorem 3.2 shows that there indeed exists a unique traffic load γ_k^* for node k to minimize its worst-case delay, and that γ_k^* is independent of the delay threshold σ, which can be also observed in Fig. 3.7. Thus, the delivery delay of messages with different delay thresholds can be all minimized at the same optimal traffic load.

3.3.2 Jamming Impact on Uncoordinated Communications

So far, we have derived the theoretical results of the worst-case jamming impact on coordinated communication, which is used for IED communication in normal operations in the smart grid. We show that, interestingly, there indeed exists a unique traffic load for a node to minimize its worst-case delay. In the following, we present the theoretical results on uncoordinated communication, which can be used for key establishment between IEDs. Similar to Sect. 3.3.1, our goal is to find out the worst case performance, $\mathbb{P}(D > \sigma)$, for uncoordinated communication under both non-reactive and reactive jamming attacks.

Theorem 3.3 (Worst Case Delay in Uncoordinated Mode). *For wireless local-area network $\mathcal{N}(m, N_f, N_c)$ under uncoordinated communication, the worst-case delay performance at node k is induced by the reactive jamming with sensing time τ sufficiently small. Specifically, the message delay D_k satisfies*

$$\mathbb{P}(D_k > \sigma) \leq \left(1 - \frac{(N_f N_c - 1)^{T_L(1-\rho)\gamma_k}}{(N_f N_c)^{T_L(1-\rho)\gamma_k + 1}} \left(1 - \frac{sT_L}{\frac{\tau N_f N_c}{1-\rho} + \rho T_L^2 \gamma_k} \right) \right)^{\sigma/T_L}, \tag{3.20}$$

where T_L is the message transmission duration, σ is the message delay threshold, $\gamma_k = \sum_{j=1, j \neq k}^{m} \lambda_j$, and λ_j is the traffic rate at node j.

Proof. Without loss if generality, assume that node 1 attempts to transmit a message with duration T_L to node 2 using the uncoordinated mode, in which nodes 1 and 2 uniformly choose a frequency-code channel to transmit and receive, respectively. They switch channels from time to time. For the sake of simplicity, the time is partitioned into time slots with length T_L. The sender and receiver switch their channels at the beginning of each time slot. Assume that for the ith delivery attempt ($1 \leq i \leq \sigma/T_L$), nodes 1 and 2 reside at the (u_i, v_i)th channel and the (d_i, e_i)th channel, respectively.

The message invalidation probability $\mathbb{P}(D_1 > \sigma)$ can be represented as

$$\mathbb{P}(D_1 > \sigma) = \mathbb{P}\left(\cap_{i=1}^{\sigma/T_L} (C_i \cup J_i \cup M_i) \right), \tag{3.21}$$

where C_i and J_i denote the events that the ith transmission is disrupted by collision and jamming, respectively; and M_i denotes the event that there is a channel mismatch between the sender and receiver, i.e., $M_i = \{u_i \neq d_i\} \cup \{v_i \neq e_i\}$.

To find $\mathbb{P}(D_1 > \sigma)$, we first need to compute the collision probability $P(C_i)$, jamming probability $P(J_i)$, and the mismatch probability $P(M_i)$, respectively. Since we have already obtained $P(C_i)$ in (3.3), as well as $P(J_i)$ in (3.5) and (3.11) under non-reactive and reactive jamming attacks, we in the following derive $P(M_i)$, which is the probability that node 1 does not reside at the same channel as node 2, i.e., either $u_i \neq d_i$ or $v_i \neq e_i$. We have

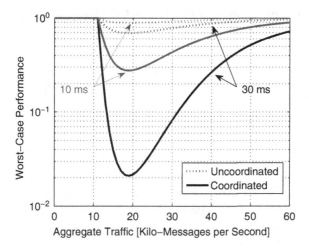

Fig. 3.9 Uncoordinated communication: worst-case $\mathbb{P}(D_k > \sigma)$ versus γ_k with delay thresholds of 10 ms and 30 ms ($N_f = 10$, $N_c = 1$, $T_L = 0.8$ ms, $\rho = 0.1$, and $\tau = 100\,\mu s$ for reactive jamming)

$$\mathbb{P}(M_i) = \mathbb{P}\left(\{u_i \neq d_i\} \cup \{v_i \neq e_i\}\right) = 1 - 1/(N_f N_c). \qquad (3.22)$$

With (3.21), (3.22), (3.3), (3.5) and (3.11), using similar procedures in Theorem 3.1, we can show $\mathbb{P}(D > \sigma)$ satisfies (3.20).   □

Figure 3.9 shows an example of the worst-case message invalidation probabilities for a time-critical application in both coordinated and uncoordinated modes. It is observed that similar to coordinated communication, the worst-case message invalidation probability in uncoordinated communication exhibits U-shaped curves in Fig. 3.9, indicating that the delay performance in uncoordinated communication also depends on the aggregate traffic load γ_k, and can be minimized by optimizing γ_k. However, the delay performance in uncoordinated communication is substantially worse than that in coordinated communication. This is due to the opportunistic nature of uncoordinated communication: the sender and receiver have to randomly select channels to transmit and receive, respectively. Figure 3.9 implies that in general, uncoordinated communication should not be used for time-critical message delivery.

Another observation in Fig. 3.9 is that the message invalidation probability is always minimized at the same traffic load regardless of communication modes. For example, we can see that the probabilities for all four cases in Fig. 3.9 are all minimized at $\gamma_k \approx 19$ kilo-messages/s. This shows that if we have the same setups in a wireless network, there exists one optimal traffic load for a node to minimize its message invalidation probability in both coordinated and uncoordinated communications, which is formally proved in the following.

Theorem 3.4 (Optimal Load in Uncoordinated Mode). *In a wireless network with setups stated in Theorem 3.2, node k's optimal load γ_k^* in coordinated mode can also minimize its message invalidation probability in uncoordinated mode.*

Proof. For uncoordinated communication, in order to minimize (3.20) (as a function of γ_k), it is equivalent to find the value of γ_k to maximize function

$$
g(\gamma_k) = \frac{(N_f N_c - 1)^{T_L(1-\rho)\gamma_k}}{(N_f N_c)^{T_L(1-\rho)\gamma_k+1}} \left(1 - \frac{(1-\rho)sT_L}{\tau N_f N_c + \rho(1-\rho)T_L^2 \gamma_k} \right)
$$
$$
= f(\gamma_k)/(N_f N_c), \tag{3.23}
$$

where $f(\gamma_k)$ is given in (3.16), which is the objective function in the coordinated mode. Hence, finding γ_k^* that maximizes $g(\gamma_k)$ is equivalent to finding γ_k^* that maximizes $f(\gamma_k)$. Therefore, γ_k^* minimizes the message invalidation probabilities in coordinated and uncoordinated modes.   □

Remark 3.4. Despite the evident performance difference between coordinated and uncoordinated communications, Theorem 3.4 illustrates that their delay performance can always be optimized at the same time by choosing one optimum traffic load in the network. In the smart grid, a node's traffic load is usually static and quite unsaturated for monitoring and control on critical power devices. For example, wireless monitoring for substation transformers only needs to transmit a message every second [6]. This indicates that in general, we should intentionally increase a certain amount of redundant traffic to obtain the optimal traffic load. Then, legitimate messages can have a chance to be successfully delivered during the period that jamming attacks attempt to disrupt redundant traffic. We name such traffic as *camouflage traffic* since it serves as camouflage to "hide" legitimate traffic from attacks.

Remark 3.5. It is worthy of mention that from the jammer's perspective, an interesting question is how to approach the worst-case performance for a particular node. Our theoretical analysis in Theorems 3.1 and 3.3 shows that the jammer must be a reactive one targeting the node, and keep sensing the channel one by one with minimum sensing time, and successfully disrupt the transmission with minimum effective duration if it senses a channel activity, then jump to the next channel to sense again.

3.4 Transmitting Adaptive Camouflage Traffic

We have shown that for both coordinated and uncoordinated communications in wireless smart grid applications, the delay performance is sensitive to the network traffic load under jamming attacks. As a result, generating camouflage traffic is promising to improve the worst-case delay performance. In this section, we present our adaptive method that generates camouflage traffic to minimize the message delivery delay in wireless networks for smart grid applications.

3.4.1 Motivation and Method Design

Our objective is to design a feasible method to minimize the worst case delay performance for practical wireless smart gird applications under jamming attacks. We first describe the general idea of our method, which can be used for both coordinated and uncoordinated communication modes. Notice that Theorem 3.2 shows that the optimal load γ_k^* is a function of message transmission time T_L, which depends on message length L. If all nodes' messages have the same length, the optimal load for every node will be the same, i.e., $\gamma_1^* = \gamma_2^* = \cdots = \gamma_m^*$. However, in the smart grid, a node has different message types with distinct lengths. For example, monitoring and control messages in substations can have lengths of 98 and 16 bytes [19], respectively. Thus, it is impossible to use one optimal load to minimize the delay for all message types. A reasonable choice is to generate camouflage traffic at the optimal point to minimize the delay for the most time-critical messages, since such messages are of the most importance and generally used for protection procedures [11, 19]. Therefore, to obtain the optimal traffic load γ_k^*, T_L is chosen to be the transmission time of the most time-critical messages. Then, we have $\gamma_1^* = \gamma_2^* = \cdots = \gamma_m^*$.

It is also worthy of mention that the optimal traffic load γ_k^* is a function of the jammer's sensing time τ. As τ varies in practice, it is difficult to pre-configure network setups to generate camouflage traffic at the optimal load. An appropriate strategy is to adaptively generate traffic at each node into the network such that the overall network traffic load can be balanced around the optimum. Thus, we design the TACT method (transmitting adaptive camouflage traffic). The intuition behind TACT is twofold.

1. TACT should avoid node coordination. Admittedly, node coordination can further help improve the delay performance. However, it introduces an additional security issue of coordination message delivery under jamming. Thus, TACT should be of distributed nature, inducing the minimum complexity and node coordination.
2. Since the worst-case message delay is minimized at a positive traffic load, TACT should always attempt to increase the traffic load. If the performance is degraded after the increase, it should reduce the traffic load.

Accordingly, we propose to implement the TACT method at every node in a wireless network for the smart grid. As shown in Algorithm 2, TACT measures the delivery results of probing messages to adjust the amount of camouflage messages in the network. Each camouflage message is transmitted on a randomly selected frequency/code channel. When TACT is deployed, there are three major traffic

---

Algorithm 2 : TACT at Each Node

Given: Camouflage traffic load L, L_{min} and L_{max}.
Given: Traffic increment Δ_{inc} and decrement Δ_{dec}.
Initialization: $M_{prev} \leftarrow 0$, $L \leftarrow L_{min}$
repeat
  Transmit probing messages in an observation period.
  Measure the number of ACKs, M_{now}.
  if Performance not degraded ($M_{now} \geq M_{prev}$) **then**
    Increase the traffic load: $L \leftarrow \min(L + \Delta_{inc}, L_{max})$.
  else
    Decrease the traffic load: $L \leftarrow \max(L - \Delta_{dec}, L_{min})$.
  end if
  Record history: $M_{prev} \leftarrow M_{now}$.
until TACT is disabled.

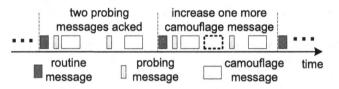

Fig. 3.10 Diagram to illustrate how TACT balances the network traffic

types in the network: (1) *routine traffic* for power monitoring and control, which cannot be changed as it is coupled with setups of power devices, (2) *probing traffic* for performance measurement, its message transmission time equals to T_L, (3) *camouflage traffic* to balance the overall network traffic load. Figure 3.10 shows an example of traffic dynamics caused by TACT: in the first observation period, two probing messages are both ACKed, meaning that current traffic load is not harmful. Then, TACT sends one more camouflage message in the next observation period. The traffic load will keep being increased until it reaches the optimum, and finally fluctuate around the optimum.

3.4.2 Uniform Optimum

When TACT is deployed at node k, it starts to increase node k's traffic load λ_k. However, increasing λ_k cannot improve node k's own delay performance since $\mathbb{P}(D_k > \sigma)$ is not a function of λ_k but a function of $\gamma_k = \sum_{j=1, j \neq k}^{m} \lambda_j$. By transmitting more traffic into the network, node k in fact improves the network traffic loads γ_i ($i \neq k$) observed at other nodes. At the same time, node k is expecting others to do the same to help itself. Thus, the efficiency of TACT relies on such homogenous behavior in all nodes, which however cannot be guaranteed when nodes have evidently heterogeneous traffic rates. Consider an extreme case: there are two nodes (nodes 1 and 2) with routine traffic rates of 1 and 1000 messages/s, respectively. The optimal loads $\gamma_1^* = \gamma_2^* = 1000$ under a reactive jammer. Initially, $\gamma_1 = \sum_{j=1, j\neq 1}^2 \lambda_j = 1000$ and $\gamma_2 = \sum_{j=1, j\neq 2}^2 \lambda_j = 1$. When TACT starts, node 2 is far from the optimum and keeps increasing its traffic load. In contrast, node 1 immediately reaches the optimum and never generates more traffic to help node 2.

Therefore, in order to ensure uniform optimum over all nodes, a solution is to mandate every node have the same minimum traffic load, regardless of their different routine traffic rates. This can be achieved by assigning different minimum camouflage traffic loads $L_{\min}$ (as given in Algorithm 2) to different nodes. Specifically, let node k's minimum camouflage traffic load $L_{\min}(k) = \max_{1\leq i\leq m} \alpha_i - \alpha_k$, where α_i denotes the (fixed) routine traffic load at node i. Thus, the minimum overall traffic load must be transmitted by every node is uniformly equal to $\max_{1\leq i\leq m} \alpha_i$. In the previous example, we can assign $L_{\min} = 999$ and 0 to nodes 1 and 2, respectively. Then, both nodes can have the optimal traffic load when TACT starts. If the optimal load is 1500 messages/s, both nodes will increase their camouflage traffic loads until reaching the optimum. In the next section, we use experiments to show the effectiveness of TACT.

3.5 Smart Grid Anti-islanding Application: Secure Key Establishment and Communication

We have found that there exists an optimal traffic load to minimize the worst-case message delay, and carefully designed the distributed TACT method to achieve the optimal load. In this section, we aim at implementing a practical TACT based system to optimize the delay performance of an important smart grid application, anti-islanding, under jamming attacks in our experimental micro smart grid, Green Hub [2].

3.5.1 Anti-islanding for an Experimental Micro Smart Grid

Our goal is to use real-world experiments to show the effectiveness of the proposed method, TACT, to improve the delay performance of a wireless application in the smart grid under jamming attacks. In the following, we first introduce the smart grid system used in the experiments. The FREEDM systems center[3] has established a micro smart grid, Green Hub [2] to test key smart grid components, such as solid-state transformer (SST) and communication infrastructure. Green Hub includes two solar-array based photovoltaic (PV) systems as distributed energy resources.

---

[3]The Future Renewable Electric Energy Delivery and Management (FREEDM) systems center at North Carolina State University, Raleigh NC.

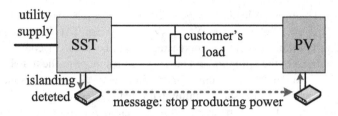

Fig. 3.11 Anti-islanding procedure in Green Hub

An important protection procedure for distritbuted energy resources is anti-islanding. In power engineering, islanding [7] refers to the condition in which distributed energy resources continue power supply even though the electric utility is disconnected. Unintentional islanding can cause many problems, such as damaging customers' loads and harming distributed energy resources [7]. Thus, anti-islanding protection procedures must be deployed in power systems to prevent any unintentional islanding.

Figure 3.11 shows an anti-island procedure in Green Hub: when the utility supply is disconnected, the SST detects the islanding and sends an anti-islanding message to the PV system to make the system stop generating power. The delay threshold of such a message is 150–300 ms [12].

3.5.2 System Setups

Network Setup There have been several wireless testing networks for anti-islanding in the power engineering community [7, 12]. In this work, we use universal software radio peripheral (USRP) devices with GNU Radio to set up a frequency-hopping based wireless network to provide jamming resilience for the anti-islanding application. Green Hub has two PV-SST pairs for anti-islanding protection. Each device is connected to an IED for communication. Thus, the network consists of four IEDs and a gateway for centralized management. Each IED's routine traffic is one message of status update to the gateway every second. Both IEDs and the gateways use USRPs to communicate with each other.

Spread Spectrum Systems The network uses eight frequency hopping channels at the 2.4 GHz band, each of which uses BPSK modulation and has a bandwidth of 125 KHz, resulting in a total network bandwidth of 1 MHz. The length of an anti-islanding message is 400 bytes, thereby leading to a transmission time of $(400*8)/125 = 25.6$ ms. The delay threshold is set to be 150 ms. The application layer at each IED transmits one message four times. Thus, the secret key shared by each transmit-receive pair is a frequency-hopping pattern with four hops. For TACT, the lengths of probing and camouflage messages are set to be 400 and 1000 bytes, respectively. Note that we choose long camouflage messages to increase the chance that a reactive jammer senses and jams such messages.

Jamming Attacks We also set up a USRP-based jammer with operational bandwidth of 125 KHz. When it is non-reactive, it keeps broadcasting jamming pulses, each of which is sent on a randomly selected channel. When it is reactive, it uses an energy detector to scan all eight hopping channels one by one, and jams any ongoing transmission as long as it senses energy activity. The jamming pulse duration is set to be 1 ms.

3.5.3   Experimental Results

When the network is set up, all IEDs need to first communicate uncoordinatedly with the gateway node to obtain their secret keys of channel assignments, then they use the keys to communicate coordinately. As a result, in the following, we first consider the uncoordinated case; i.e., we first evaluate how TACT can improve the delay performance of key establishment, and then move on to the coordinated case.

3.5.3.1   Key Establishment

In this experiment, we consider the uncoordinated communication for key establishment: every node attempts to communicate with the gateway by keeping sending key requests on uniformly selected frequency channels. At the same time, the gateway also uniformly chooses a frequency channel to receive. The delivery of a message is successful only when a node and the gateway reside on the same channel. We define the delay of the key establishment for a node is the time duration from the instant that the node sends the first key request to the instant that the node receives the reply from the gateway.

Figure 3.12 illustrates the mean delay of key establishment as a function of the network traffic load under both non-reactive jamming and reactive jamming. We can observe from Fig. 3.12 that reactive jamming always induces larger key establishment delay than non-reactive jamming for uncoordinate communication, which indicates that we should always consider the reactive jamming as the worst-case scenario for uncoordinate communication. Note that Fig. 3.12 exhibits a U-shaped curve for the delay performance under reactive jamming, showing that under reactive jamming, there always exists a traffic load to minimize the average key establishment delay. As a result, TACT that is primarily designed to counter-attack reactive jamming by achieving the optimal traffic load, should be useful to substantially decrease the key establishment delay in our experiential wireless network.

Next, we enable TACT at every node and evaluate the effectiveness of TACT on uncoordinated communication under reactive jamming. During experiments, we set the following TACT parameters: $L_{min}=0$, $L_{max}=30$, $\Delta_{inc}=2$, $\Delta_{dec}=2$, and ten probing messages are sent every second. Table 3.1 illustrates the average key establishment delay under three scenarios: (1) frequency hopping under reactive jamming (TACT

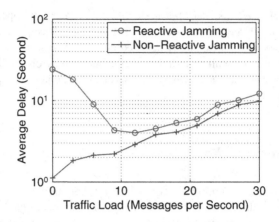

Fig. 3.12 Uncoordinated: average key establishment delay versus per-node network traffic load

Table 3.1 Average delay in uncoordinated communication

Setups	TACT off	TACT on	Baseline
Delay	24.2 s	5.61 s	0.814 s

is off), (2) frequency hopping with camouflage traffic (TACT is on), (3) baseline performance (no jamming, no TACT). It is observed from Table 3.1 that uncoordinated communication based key establishment incurs fairly large delay even for the baseline (no-jamming case) performance that have the average delay of 814 ms. This is due to the opportunistic nature of uncoordinated communication. Under reactive jamming attacks, we can see that the key establishment delay increases to 24.2 s. However, when TACT is enabled, the delay decreases dramatically to 5.61 s, as shown in Table 3.1. Therefore, TACT is an effective measure to improve the key establishment delay performance for wireless smart grid applications.

3.5.3.2 Jamming-Resilient Communication

In this experiment, we consider the coordinated communication mode after the key has been established. We evaluate the impact of both reactive and non-reactive jammers on the anti-island application. We generate camouflage messages at fixed rates of 0–30 messages/s at each IED. Figure 3.13 shows that the message invalidation probability for anti-islanding messaging as a function of the camouflage traffic rate of each IED. We can see from Fig. 3.13 that reactive jamming always leads to worse performance than non-reactive jamming, indicating that we should always consider the reactive jamming as the worst-case scenario. Thus, in the following, we will only consider the reactive jamming. Figure 3.13 also shows that the message invalidation probability induced by reactive jamming is a U-shaped

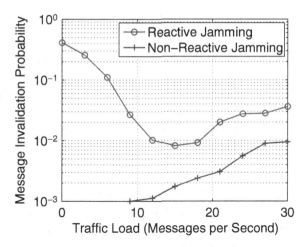

Fig. 3.13 Coordinated: message invalidation probability versus traffic load

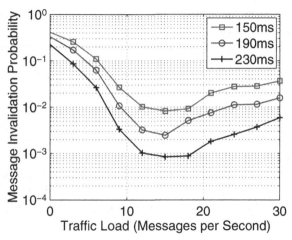

Fig. 3.14 Coordinated: message invalidation probability with different delay thresholds

function of the traffic load. We can see that the message invalidation probability decreases from 41.2 to 0.82 % as the camouflage traffic load goes from 0 to 15 messages/s.

Then, we consider the delay performance with different delay thresholds of 150, 190, and 230 ms under reactive jamming. If the delay threshold becomes larger, we can transmit the same message more times to ensure more reliability. Thus, the transmissions have five, six, and seven hops (transmission attempts) for messages with delay thresholds of 150, 190, and 230 ms, respectively. Figure 3.14 shows that the message invalidation probabilities for different delay thresholds. We can observe that the minimum probabilities are always achieved at 15 messages/s, which in turn indicates that the optimal traffic load is independent of the delay threshold.

Next, we evaluate the effectiveness of TACT against reactive jamming in coordinated communication. We use the same setups in Table 3.1. Table 3.2 illustrates

Table 3.2 Message invalidation in coordinated communication

Setups	TACT off	TACT on	Baseline
Delay	41.2 %	0.9076 %	0.0532 %

Table 3.3 Message invalidation vs the number of hopping channels

Number of channels (N_f)	6	8	10	12
TACT off	92.3 %	68.1 %	41.2 %	10.1 %
TACT on	15.1 %	6.01 %	0.831 %	0.212 %

message invalidation probabilities in three scenarios: (1) frequency hopping under reactive jamming (TACT is off), (2) frequency hopping with camouflage traffic (TACT is on), (3) baseline performance (no jamming, no TACT). It is observed from Table 3.2 that TACT decreases the message invalidation probability from 41.2 to 0.9076 %. Although TACT does not achieve the minimum probability of 0.82 % shown in Fig. 3.13, it still improves the delay performance in order of magnitude under reactive jamming. Note that the baseline performance in Table 3.2 shows a positive message invalidation probability. This is because error correction is not used in our experiments in order to reduce the GNU Radio processing delay.

Table 3.3 shows the message invalidation probability as a function of the number of frequency-hopping channels N_f under reactive jamming. It is known that increasing N_f can reduce the message delay for spread spectrum communication, as more spectrum resources are used. Table 3.3 illustrates that when N_f goes from 6 to 12, the message invalidation probability in the frequency-hopping-only (no TACT) scenario decreases from 92.3 to 10.1 %; while TACT can further reduce the probability from 10.1 to 0.21 %. As a result, TACT is a promising mechanism that offers a new dimension to improve the delay performance for smart grid communication.

3.6 Summary

In this chapter, we provided a comprehensive study on minimizing the message delay for smart grid applications under jamming attacks. By defining a generic jamming process, we showed that the worst-case message delay is a U-shaped function of network traffic load. We designed a distributed method, TACT, to generate camouflage traffic to balance the network load at the optimal point. We implemented TACT for the anti-islanding application in Green Hub, and showed that TACT is a promising method to significantly improve the delay performance in the smart grid under jamming attacks.

References

1. Akyol B, Kirkham H, Clements S, Hadley M (2010) A survey of wireless communications for the electric power system. Technical Report, Pacific Northwest National Laboratory
2. Baran M, Shen Z, Liu Z (2010) Power management strategies for the Green Hub. In: FREEDM systems center annual conference
3. Bayraktaroglu E, King C, Liu X, Noubir G, Rajaraman R, Thapa B (2008) On the performance of IEEE 802.11 under jamming. In: Proceedings of IEEE INFOCOM '08, pp 1265–1273
4. Chiang JT, Hu YC (2008) Dynamic jamming mitigation for wireless broadcast networks. In: Proceedings of IEEE INFOCOM '08
5. Cleveland F (2007) Enhancing the reliability and security of the information infrastructure used to manage the power system. In: Proceedings of the IEEE power & energy society general meeting (PES '07)
6. Cleveland F (2007) Uses of wireless communications to enhance power system reliability. In: Proceedings of the IEEE power & energy society general meeting (PES '07)
7. El-Khattam W, Sidhu TS, Seethapathy R (2010) Evaluation of two anti-islanding schemes for a radial distribution system equipped with self-excited induction generator wind turbines. IEEE Trans Energy Convers 25:107–117
8. Gardner J (2011) Spread spectrum communications for SCADA systems. Pipeline Gas J 238: 1–6
9. Glisic SG, Mammela A, Kaasila VP, Pajkovic MD (1995) Rejection of frequency sweeping signal in DS spread spectrum systems using complex adaptive filters. IEEE Trans Commun 43(1):136–145
10. Goldsmith A (2005) Wireless communications. Cambridge University Press, Cambridge
11. IEC Standard (2003) IEC 61850: communication networks and systems in substations
12. Kanabar PM, Kanabar MG, El-Khattam W, Sidhu TS, Shami A (2009) Evaluation of communication technologies for IEC 61850 based distribution automation system with distributed energy resources. In: Proceedings of the IEEE power & energy society general meeting (PES '09)
13. Li H, Lai L, Qiu RC (2011) A denial-of-service jamming game for remote state monitoring in smart grid. In: Proceedings of 45th annual conference on information sciences and systems (CISS)
14. Liu Y, Ning P, Dai H, Liu A (2010) Randomized differential DSSS: jamming-resistant wireless broadcast communication. In: Proceedings of IEEE INFOCOM'10
15. Lu X, Wang W, Ma J (2012) Authentication and integrity in the smart grid: an empirical study in substation automation systems. Int J Distrib Sens Netw 2012:1–13
16. Mohagheghi S, Stoupis J, Wang Z (2009) Communication protocols and networks for power systems - current status and future trends. In: Proceedings of power systems conference and exposition (PES '09)
17. Popper C, Strasser M, Capkun S (2009) Jamming-resistant broadcast communication without shared keys. In: Proceedings of USENIX security symposium (Security '09)
18. Pöpper C, Strasser M, Čapkun S (2010) Anti-jamming broadcast communication using uncoordinated spread spectrum techniques. IEEE J Sel Areas Commun (Special Issue on Mission Critical Networking, IEEE) 28:703–715
19. Sidhu TS, Yin Y (2007) Modelling and simulation for performance evaluation of IEC61850-based substation communication systems. IEEE Trans Power Deliv 22(3):1482–1489
20. Strasser M, Capkun S, Popper C, Cagalj M (2008) Jamming-resistant key establishment using uncoordinated frequency hopping. In: Proceedings of IEEE symposium on security and privacy, pp 64–78
21. Strasser M, Popper C, Capkun S (2009) Efficient uncoordinated FHSS anti-jamming communication. In: Proceedings of MobiHoc '09
22. The Smart Grid Interoperability Panel - Cyber Security Working Group (2010) Guidelines for smart grid cyber security. NIST IR-7628 1–3

23. Wang W, Xu Y, Khanna M (2011) A survey on the communication architectures in smart grid. Comput Netw 55:3604–3629
24. Wilhelm M, Martinovic I, Schmitt JB, Lenders V (2011) Short paper: reactive jamming in wireless networks: how realistic is the threat? In: Proceedings of ACM conference on wireless security (WiSec)
25. Xu W, Trappe W, Zhang Y, Wood T (2005) The feasibility of launching and detecting jamming attacks in wireless networks. In: Proceedings of ACM MobiHoc '05, pp 46–57

Chapter 4
Understanding the Resilience of Mobile Cloud Services to Malware

4.1 Introduction

With the proliferation of smart handheld devices and ubiquitous wireless network connectivity, mobile cloud computing [2, 18] emerges as a computing paradigm for mobile applications, in which computationally intensive tasks in capability-limited mobile nodes are moved via wireless access networks to a data center, called *the cloud*, for centralized, efficient processing. Such a new computing model is envisioned to solve long-standing issues related to performance bottlenecks in conventional mobile applications, such as real-time services [1, 22] and energy issues [8, 18].

However, together with its benefits, mobile cloud computing also faces significant security challenges [10]. In particular, with the advancement of flexible mobile platforms and software, mobile malware [10, 16], which is malicious software targeting mobile applications, no longer occurs in theory. In fact, statistics show that mobile malware has exploded in recent years. For example, from 2010 to 2011, mobile malware samples had exceeded 1300 with a more than 100 % increase [20] overall and a 400 % increase in Android platforms [14]. Worldwide, the likelihood of encountering mobile malware in 2011 varies from less than 1 % to more than 4 % depending on country [19]. As a result, mobile malware has become *de facto* the primary threat to mobile applications, in particular to the emerging mobile cloud market [7].

Mobile malware can lead to a wide range of impacts on mobile applications, such as information leakage and blocking the use of mobile devices [10]. Recently, there is an increased concern over denial-of-service impacts caused by malware on mobile cloud services [3, 17] since malware has already shown the ability to compromise a non-negligible number of mobile devices in a short time period, and command them to effectively launch coordinated attacks [21, 26]. Despite such impendent threats in practice, little attention has been focused on analyzing denial-of-service impacts

© The Author(s) 2015
Z. Lu et al., *Modeling and Evaluating Denial of Service Attacks for Wireless and Mobile Applications*, SpringerBriefs in Computer Science,
DOI 10.1007/978-3-319-23288-1_4

of malware on mobile cloud services in the literature. As a result, it is still unclear *how resilient (or vulnerable) mobile cloud services are to malware attacks*. The answer to this question is vital to help us understand how mobile malware attacks affect cloud service delivery to mobile users. In addition, it can provide guidance into design of countermeasures for mobile cloud services against malware attacks.

In this work, we aim to *quantify the resilience of mobile cloud services to malware attacks*. As mobile cloud computing is intended to provide real-time services/applications to mobile users (e.g., interactive perception applications [22], advanced navigation [1], and application/code offload [8, 27]), service requests from legitimate users are expected to be processed and returned by the cloud in a timely manner. Accordingly, to measure the resilience of mobile cloud services to malware attacks, we define a new performance metric, *resilience factor*, which denotes the maximally allowable percentage of malware-infected nodes in the network such that a required ratio of cloud service requests from legitimate users can still be processed on time.

Based on the metric of resilience factor, we measure the malware resilience of mobile cloud services via both theoretical analysis and comprehensive experiments in our small-scale cloud, which is built upon open-source cloud computing frameworks to process service requests for mobile users. The major findings are twofold.

1. We show that for a mobile cloud service, there exists a cutoff point B^* on network bandwidth B. If $B < B^*$, we say the service is in the *network-limited region*, in which the resilience factor is an *increasing* function of B; on the other hand, if $B > B^*$, we say the service is in the *cloud-limited region*, in which the resilience factor *decreases* on the order of $1/B$.
2. We find that in malware epidemics (i.e., in the scenario where the malware-infected nodes are launching denial-of-service attacks), if the mobile cloud service is in the network-limited region, low service quality is mainly caused by local network congestion especially at mobility hotspots, the cloud is in fact fairly or even lightly loaded, thereby resulting in heterogeneous malware resilience across the network; if the mobile cloud service is in the cloud-limited region, cloud overload becomes the dominant factor for performance degradation, which can also lead to global service failure.

The dichotomy of the resilience factor on the network bandwidth demonstrates a *negative* perspective on developing network infrastructures for emerging mobile cloud services: on one hand, increasing network bandwidth is considered necessary for current cellular networks to support mobile cloud services [9, 13]; on the other hand, it can substantially decrease the resilience factor, thereby raising the chance of global service failure in malware epidemics. In addition, our results indicate that countermeasures should be deployed in both the network and cloud for effectively combating malware attacks to protect mobile cloud services, which can be in either network-limited or cloud-limited regions.

The rest of this chapter is organized as follows. In Sect. 4.2, we introduce preliminaries and models used in this chapter. In Sects. 4.3 and 4.4, we measure the resilience factor for mobile cloud services via analysis and experiments. We summarize and discuss our results in Sect. 4.5 and finally conclude in Sect. 4.6.

4.2 Preliminaries and Models

In this section, we first present network, service and attack models, then introduce the metric of resilience factor.

4.2.1 Network and Mobile Users

Mobile cloud computing in general refers to an infrastructure where data storage and processing happen outside of mobile devices [2, 9]. In other words, mobile nodes will send their data to the cloud for processing or storage. Accordingly, to support mobile cloud computing, there must be two distinct types of nodes in the network: mobile nodes that are common users, and cloud nodes that provide cloud services/connections to mobile nodes.

Therefore, we consider a hybrid wireless network that consists of both cloud nodes and mobile nodes to support mobile cloud services, as shown in Fig. 4.1.

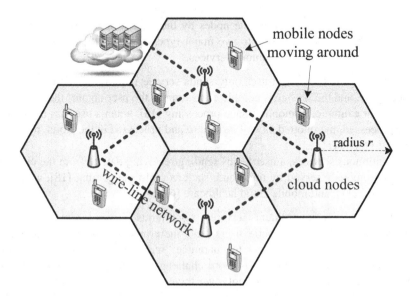

Fig. 4.1 Network architecture: cloud nodes and mobile nodes

Cloud nodes are interconnected with each other via high-speed wireline networks such that they can either form a cloud or connected to a cloud center to process service requests from mobile nodes. They also have the wireless network interface that offers wireless access to mobile nodes. Like the deployment in cellular networks (e.g. 3G/4G), cloud nodes form hexagonal cells with radius r in the network in order to fully cover a wide range of areas.

Mobile nodes move around in the network, communicating with their nearest cloud nodes for cloud services. The transmission range of mobile nodes is the same as the transmission range of cloud nodes, and the network bandwidth B is shared among all mobile and cloud nodes. Mobile nodes consist of legitimate nodes that continuously request the cloud service from the cloud, and malicious nodes that are compromised by malware and attempt to disrupt the cloud service. Since statistics have already shown that as of today a non-negligible portion (e.g., 1–4 % [19]) of smart phones are infected by malware, we assume that a portion $\rho \in (0,1)$ of all mobile nodes are compromised by malware, where ρ is called *malware infection ratio*. Let n be the number of mobile nodes in the network. Then, we represent the network as $\mathcal{N}(n,\rho,B)$.

Both legitimate and malware-infected nodes are mobile. We assume that malware can only compromise a node's information system, but cannot decide the node's movement since mobility is usually determined by human being.

4.2.2 Mobile Cloud Services

To understand how resilient mobile cloud services are to malware, we need to know what services are offered to mobile nodes by the cloud. Hence, we first classify existing mobile cloud services into two major types based on their network traffic patterns: intermittent and continuous services.

- In intermittent services, a user only sends service requests to the cloud when necessary, and the service is completed as long as the user obtains the processed data. For example, in mobile image processing [18], when a user has a photo to be processed, the photo data will be sent to and processed in the cloud, then sent back to the user.
- In continuous services, a user keeps sending/receiving data to/from the cloud to be continuously served by the cloud, such as real-time gaming [18], advanced navigation [1], and mobile cloud healthcare [6].

Compared with intermittent services, continuous services aim at offering real-time applications to mobile users, and therefore need service requests to be processed in a timely manner to guarantee "real-time-ness" [1, 6, 18]. Thus, maintaining continuous services is more challenging and resource-demanding in mobile cloud computing. Accordingly, we focus on continuous cloud services in this chapter.

We represent a continuous service as $\S(l_s, l_r, f, \sigma)$: a node sends packets with size l_s bits to the cloud at a constant rate of f packets per second, and receives packets containing processed data with size l_r bits at the same rate. In addition, each service request has a latency requirement of σ seconds. For example, in a cloud-assisted navigation system [18], the navigator can send its GPS coordinates to the cloud every second, then expects to receive path correction or points-of-interest information within several hundreds of milliseconds.

4.2.3 Malware Attack Model

We have defined how mobile nodes communicate with the cloud for continuous service $\S(l_s, l_r, f, \sigma)$. When a node is infected by malware, it may not behave legitimately according to the service specification. In general, mobile malware is malicious software on mobile devices that has distinct behaviors and can lead to either individual or global impacts [10, 21].

- Individual impact. This type of malware can block the use or take control of mobile devices, or acquire individual's private information (e.g., Spitmo and Zeusmitmo [10]).
- Global impact. If mobile nodes are infected by the same malware, they can in fact form a mobile botnet [21, 26], which is a collection of compromised mobile devices targeting the same victim. Nowadays, the threat of mobile botnets is indeed real. For example [21], in November 2009, a mobile worm named *Ikee.A* infected around 21,000 iPhones within 2 weeks by simply copying itself through a security vulnerability. Then, by a simple command and control mechanism, *Ikee.A* was turned into botnet *Ikee.B* that was able to command thousands of compromised devices to attack one single target.

From the perspective of reliable system operations, the issue of mobile botnets is more challenging than that of malware with individual impacts. Therefore, we focus on dealing with malware-infected nodes that form a botnet with the goal to launch denial-of-service attacks. In particular, we assume that in network $\mathcal{N}(n, \rho, B)$, all the $n\rho$ malware-infected nodes form a botnet and have the same target, i.e., the cloud. Unlike legitimate nodes that request the cloud service at a constant rate of f, malware-infected nodes will saturate their network interfaces by keeping sending service processing requests with size l_s via the wireless access network to the cloud. In other words, malware-infected nodes, by flooding much more service requests to the cloud, aim to disrupt the cloud service for all legitimate nodes.

Remark 4.1. The impacts of such malware on mobile cloud services are twofold: (1) it can lead to network congestion in the wireless access network that is shared among all contending users [26]; (2) it floods service requests to the cloud, making the cloud heavily loaded and slower to respond to legitimate service requests [3].

4.2.4 *Metric to Measure Malware Resilience*

In order to quantify the resilience of mobile cloud services under malware attacks, it is necessary to first understand how to measure the performance of mobile cloud services. For continuous service $\S(l_s, l_r, f, \sigma)$, it is important to know how well the service is delivered during the service period. In other words, whether cloud service delay D, which is defined as *the time duration from the instant that a node starts to send a service request to the instant that the node finishes receiving the processed result from the cloud*, is smaller than delay requirement σ is essential for performance evaluation in real-time continuous services. If D is larger than σ, the processed information can become obsolete and useless for the node, such as in cloud-assisted navigation systems [1, 18]. Consequently, we use service on-time probability $\mathbb{P}(D \leq \sigma)$ to measure the performance of mobile cloud services.

In malware epidemics (i.e., when malware-infected nodes are launching denial-of-service attacks), malware, by keeping infecting more nodes and launching denial-of-service attacks, can gradually reduce service on-time probability $\mathbb{P}(D \leq \sigma)$ for legitimate services. This means that for given quality-of-service requirement $\theta \in (0,1)$ (i.e., the service requires $\mathbb{P}(D \leq \sigma) \geq \theta$), there should exist a critical ratio ρ^* as malware-infection ratio ρ increases from 0 such that the quality-of-service requirement cannot be satisfied when $\rho > \rho^*$. We call such a critical ratio *resilience factor*, which is in essence the maximally allowable malware-infection ratio in the network such that $\mathbb{P}(D \leq \sigma)$ can still be larger than service requirement θ. We formally define the metric of resilience factor as follows.

Definition 4.1 (Resilience Factor). In the network $\mathcal{N}(n, \rho, B)$ with cloud service $\S(l_s, l_r, f, \sigma)$, the resilience factor, denoted by $\mathscr{R}(\theta)$, is defined as the supremum of the set of malware-infection ratios ρ, with which a legitimate node's service on-time probability $\mathbb{P}(D \leq \sigma)$ is no less than quality-of-service requirement $\theta \in (0,1)$, i.e.,

$$\mathscr{R}(\theta) = \sup\{\rho \in (0,1) : \mathbb{P}(D \leq \sigma) \geq \theta\}. \tag{4.1}$$

Remark 4.2. Given quality-of-service requirement θ, the resilience factor $\mathscr{R}(\theta)$ shows the maximally allowable malware-infection ratio in the network. For example, if the requirement is set to be $\theta = 99\%$ and we find $\mathscr{R}(99\%) = 5\%$, we can know that at least 99 % service requests from legitimate nodes can be processed on time as long as malware infection ratio ρ is smaller than 5 %.

Based on Definition 4.1, we will use the resilience factor to measure the malware resilience of mobile cloud services in the following sections.

4.3 Characterizing the Malware Resilience

In this section, we present the theoretical results on the malware resilience of mobile cloud services.

4.3.1 Measuring the Cloud Processing Capability

To theoretically obtain the resilience factor, we first need to derive service on-time probability $\mathbb{P}(D \leq \sigma)$ according to Definition 4.1, where cloud service delay D consists of both network delivery delay and cloud processing delay. Suppose that if the cloud had infinite power, the processing delay would be zero, indicating that any service request can be instantly processed by the cloud. Unfortunately, existing works have already shown that the cloud processing delay is never a negligible effect. For example, 1-month data samples in commercial clouds [12] show that the running time of a Python script in Google APP Engine ranges from 1.0 to 999.7 ms. Hence, measuring the cloud processing delay is a vital part to characterize malware resilience in mobile cloud services.

In the network shown in Fig. 4.1, cloud nodes can form a cloud themselves, or maintain high-bandwidth connections to a remote cloud center to provide cloud service $\S(l_s, l_r, f, \sigma)$. Either way, when a legitimate or malware-infected node's request is delivered to a cloud node, it will be immediately processed by the cloud/parallel computing paradigm [25, 28]: the data processing will be partitioned into different tasks, which are assigned to distinct computing units; then outputs of all tasks are combined and returned to the user.

At first glance, it appears that performance modeling for cloud processing is similar to conventional queueing modeling, in which one or few users can be served and the others are waiting in the queue. Nonetheless, cloud processing can be quite different in that the cloud supports concurrent processing [5, 28] as shown in Fig. 4.2: when a user's service request arrives, the cloud can directly allocate the shared computational resources (e.g., CPU time) for it instead of making the

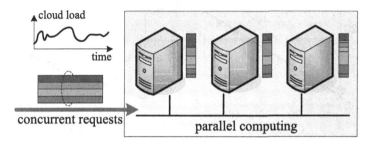

Fig. 4.2 The cloud: a cluster of computers with parallel computing ability to process a large number of user requests at the same time

user waiting. Such a concurrent processing mechanism is widely used in current cloud processing frameworks [11, 24]. Therefore, a large amount of concurrent service requests can be processed in the cloud at the same time, Intuitively, the more the concurrent users (the heavier the cloud load), the longer the processing delay. To find out the relation between the cloud processing delay and the number of concurrent users, we adopt an experimental approach in a small-scale cloud based on the Hadoop and Storm platforms.

- Hadoop [11] is an open-source cloud computing framework that allows for the processing of large data sets across clusters of computers. Hadoop is now widely used in Google, Yahoo and Facebook.
- Storm [24] is another open-source distributed computation framework, aimed at offering real-time data processing capabilities. Storm is also deployed in many commercial websites, such as Twitter and Groupon.

We set up a small-scale cloud consisting of up to eight computers with Intel Core i5 2.67 GHz. The cloud is installed with Hadoop 1.0.2 and Storm 0.70. Figure 4.3 shows the processing delay D_p as a function of constant cloud load L (which is the number of concurrent service requests being processed in the cloud at the same time) for different numbers of computers M. We can observe that for both Hadoop-based and Storm-based systems, there is approximately a linear relation between D_p and L, i.e., $D_p \approx kL$, where the slope k is a decreasing function of M, showing that the more the computing resources in the cloud, the less the processing delay. Accordingly, we assume that $D_p = kL$ for any constant load L, and define $C = 1/k$ as the cloud capability, which can be considered as an indicator to represent the maximum number of service requests that can be finished in the cloud per second. On the

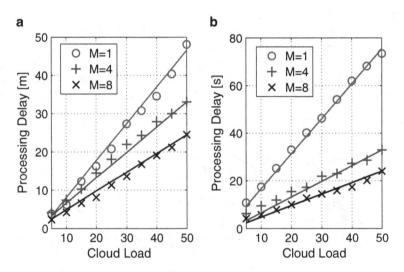

Fig. 4.3 The processing delay as a function of constant cloud load L in Hadoop and Storm with different numbers of computers M used in the cloud. (**a**) Hadoop. (**b**) Storm

other hand, in practice, every cloud must have a load limit L_{max} such that when the cloud is overloaded, it should not accept any more service requests in order to keep the system stable (e.g., parameters *poolMaxJobsDefault* and *userMaxJobsDefault* in Hadoop [11]). With parameters C and L_{max}, we define the cloud processing model as follows.

Definition 4.2 (Cloud Processing Model). The cloud processing model is denoted as $\mathscr{C}(C, L_{max})$, where C is the cloud capability, i.e., the maximum number of service requests that can be finished in the cloud every second, and L_{max} is the cloud load limit. If the cloud has a constant load $L \leq L_{max}$, the processing delay is $D_p = L/C$. When the cloud load reaches L_{max}, it will reject incoming service requests.

Remark 4.3. In practice, due to network traffic dynamics, the cloud load L is a stochastic process over time t, making the processing delay D_p a random variable. It has been shown [15, 25] that in the cloud, the selection of task schedulers (e.g., fair or coupling schedulers in Hadoop [11]), which coordinate and manage all the processes of computational tasks, can affect the stochastic property of the processing delay. To mitigate the dependence of our results on a particular task scheduler, Definition 4.2 in fact provides generic bounds for the random processing delay D_p, i.e., D_p satisfies $1/C \leq D_p \leq L_{max}/C$, which is sufficient for our later analysis.

4.3.2 Analysis of the Resilience Factor

With Definition 4.2, we start to analyze the resilience factor for cloud service $\S(l_s, l_r, f, \sigma)$. According to Definition 4.1, resilience factor $\mathscr{R}(\theta)$ is defined based on service on-time probability $\mathbb{P}(D \leq \sigma)$, or complementarily, service over-due probability $\mathbb{P}(D > \sigma)$. There are two scenarios that can result in event $\{D > \sigma\}$ happening: (1) a service request is rejected because the cloud load reaches the maximum L_{max} when it arrives, which can be regarded as the case that the service delay D is larger than σ since the request is never be processed; (2) the service is accepted by the cloud, but the sum of network and cloud processing delays is larger than σ. As a result, we first derive the property of the probability that a service request is rejected by the cloud.

Lemma 4.1. *Let R be the event that a request is rejected because the load is the maximum L_{max} when the request arrives at the cloud, then it holds for $\mathbb{P}(R)$ that*

$$1 - \frac{L_{max} l_s C}{\rho \beta B} \leq \mathbb{P}(R) \leq \frac{L_{max}(B\rho n/l_s + (1-\rho)nf)}{L_{max}(B\rho n/l_s + (1-\rho)nf) + C},$$

where $\beta \in (0, 1)$ is a constant.

Proof (Sketch). Consider a simple mechanism, in which we reject every request if a cloud with capability C/L_{max} is only loaded. Define R' as the event that a request is rejected under such a mechanism. It can be shown that $\mathbb{P}(R) \leq \mathbb{P}(R')$. Construct

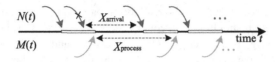

Fig. 4.4 Renewal processes $N(t)$ and $M(t)$

renewal processes $N(t)$ and $M(t)$ shown in Fig. 4.4 with renewal intervals X_{arrival} and X_{process} to denote the numbers of service request arrivals and processed service requests in the cloud under such a mechanism, respectively.

It holds for $\mathbb{P}(R')$ that $\mathbb{P}(R') = \lim_{t\to\infty} 1 - M(t)/N(t) = 1 - \lim_{t\to\infty}(M(t)/t)/(N(t)/t)$. From the property of renewal processes, we have

$$\lim_{t\to\infty} M(t)/t = 1/\mathbb{E}(X_{\text{process}}) \geq \frac{1}{L_{\max}/C + \mathbb{E}(X_{\text{arrival}})} \tag{4.2}$$

$$\lim_{t\to\infty} N(t)/t = 1/\mathbb{E}(X_{\text{arrival}}) \leq (\rho n/\mathbb{E}(D_u) + (1-\rho)nf, \tag{4.3}$$

where $\mathbb{E}(D_u)$ is the average uplink (mobile-to-cloud) delay, and clearly $\mathbb{E}(D_u) \geq l_s/B$. From (4.2) and (4.3), we obtain

$$\mathbb{P}(R) \leq \mathbb{P}(R') \leq \frac{L_{\max}(B\rho n/l_s + (1-\rho)nf)}{L_{\max}(B\rho n/l_s + (1-\rho)nf) + C}. \tag{4.4}$$

Using a similar procedure, we can obtain $\mathbb{P}(R) \geq 1 - L_{\max} C\mathbb{E}(D_u)/(\rho n)$. To derive an upper bound of $\mathbb{E}(D_u)$, consider the worst-case scenario where all n nodes move into a single cell and contend for the channel. If the access scheme in the network is TDMA (used in current cellular networks), $\mathbb{E}(D_u) \leq l_s/(B/2n)$. If the access scheme is CSMA/CA, it has been shown that by adjusting the contention window size, all competing nodes can equally share the channel and the total achievable throughput is comparable to the bandwidth B [4]. This indicates that $\mathbb{E}(D_u) \approx l_s/(\beta B/n)$ for some constant $\beta \in (0,1)$ depending on CSMA/CA schemes (e.g., $\beta \approx 0.83$ for IEEE 802.11 distributed coordination function [4]). Therefore, we can write $\mathbb{E}(D_u) = l_s n/(\beta B)$, and obtain

$$\mathbb{P}(R) \geq 1 - L_{\max} C\mathbb{E}(D_u)/(\rho n) = 1 - L_{\max} C l_s/(\rho \beta B). \tag{4.5}$$

Combining (4.4) and (4.5) completes the proof. $\qquad\square$

With Lemma 4.1, we formally state our main analytical results on the resilience factor in the following.

Theorem 4.1. *In network $\mathcal{N}(n,\rho,B)$ with cloud processing model $\mathscr{C}(C,L_{\max})$ and service $\S(l_s,l_r,f,\sigma)$, given quality-of-service requirement $\theta \in (0,1)$, resilience factor $\mathscr{R}(\theta)$ satisfies*

$$\mathscr{R}(\theta) = \begin{cases} \min\left(\Theta(B^a), 1\right), & \text{if } C = \Theta(B^{1+a}) \\ \Theta\left(1/B^a\right), & \text{if } C = \Theta(B^{1-a}) \end{cases} \tag{4.6}$$

for any positive constant $a > 0$.

Proof. Let R be the event that a service request is rejected by the cloud because the load reaches the maximum $L_{\max}$. When R is true, we have $\mathbb{P}(D > \sigma | R) = 1$ since a request will never be processed on time. When R^c is true, its cloud service delay D consists of three components, uplink delay (mobile-to-cloud) D_u, downlink delay (cloud-to-mobile) D_d, and cloud processing delay D_p. Then, $\mathbb{P}(D > \sigma)$ can be represented as

$$\mathbb{P}(D > \sigma) = \mathbb{P}(D > \sigma | R)\mathbb{P}(R) + \mathbb{P}(D > \sigma | R^c)\mathbb{P}(R^c) \tag{4.7}$$

$$\geq \mathbb{P}(R) \geq 1 - L_{\max} l_s C / (B\beta\rho),$$

where the last inequality follows from Lemma 4.1. Let $R_u(\theta) = \sup\{\rho \in (0,1) : \{1 - L_{\max} l_s C / (B\beta\rho) < 1 - \theta\}$. Then $R_u(\theta) \geq \mathscr{R}(\theta)$, and we can have $R_u(\theta) = \min(l_s C / (B\theta), 1)$. If $C = \Theta(B^{1-a})$ and $C = \Theta(B^{1+a})$, we can obtain $R_u(\theta) = \Theta(1/b^a)$ and $R_u(\theta) = \Theta(b^a)$, respectively. Therefore,

$$\mathscr{R}(\theta) \leq R_u(\theta) = \begin{cases} \min\left(\Theta(B^a), 1\right), & \text{if } C = \Theta(B^{1+a}) \\ \Theta\left(1/B^a\right), & \text{if } C = \Theta(B^{1-a}) \end{cases}. \tag{4.8}$$

On the other hand, it follows from (4.7), Markov's inequality, and Lemma 4.1 that

$$\mathbb{P}(D > \sigma) \leq \mathbb{P}(R) + \frac{\mathbb{E}(D_u) + \mathbb{E}(D_p) + \mathbb{E}(D_d)}{\sigma}(1 - \mathbb{P}(R))$$

$$\leq \mathbb{P}(R) + \frac{\mathbb{E}(D_u) + \mathbb{E}(D_d) + \mathbb{E}(D_p)}{\sigma}.$$

$$\leq \frac{\frac{B\rho n}{l_s} + (1-\rho)nf}{\frac{B\rho n}{l_s} + (1-\rho)nf) + \frac{C}{L_{\max}}} + \frac{(l_s + l_r)nC + L_{\max}\beta B}{\sigma\beta BC}.$$

Let $R_l(\theta) = \sup\{\rho \in (0,1) : \frac{L_{\max}(B\rho n/l_s + (1-\rho)nf)}{L_{\max}(B\rho n/l_s + (1-\rho)nf) + C} + \frac{(l_s + l_r)n}{\beta B\sigma} + \frac{L_{\max}}{\sigma C} < 1 - \theta\}$. Then $R_l(\theta) \leq \mathscr{R}(\theta)$, and by solving $R_l(\theta)$, we get

$$\mathscr{R}(\theta) \geq R_l(\theta) = \begin{cases} \min\left(\Theta(B^a), 1\right), & \text{if } C = \Theta(B^{1+a}) \\ \Theta\left(1/B^a\right), & \text{if } C = \Theta(B^{1-a}) \end{cases}. \tag{4.9}$$

Combining (4.8) and (4.9) finishes the proof. $\qquad\square$

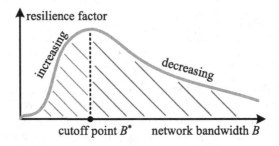

Fig. 4.5 The resilience factor as a function of the network bandwidth

The results in Theorem 4.1 are general since there is no further assumptions on network access schemes (e.g., TDMA and CSMA/CA), node mobility or cloud task scheduling mechanisms. There are two key observations from Theorem 4.1.

1. If cloud capability C is on the higher order of network bandwidth B (i.e., $C = \Theta(B^{1+a})$), we can see in Theorem 4.1 that the resilience factor $\mathscr{R}(\theta) = \min(\Theta(B^a), 1)$, which is an increasing function of B. This means that we will obtain 100 % malware resilience when B is sufficiently large. Therefore, such a result indicates that strong malware resilience is possible for mobile cloud services.

2. In a practical scenario where cloud capability C is always finite (i.e., C is a constant denoted by $\Theta(1)$), the resilience factor satisfies $\mathscr{R}(\theta) = \Theta(1/B)$ according to Theorem 4.1, showing that $\mathscr{R}(\theta)$ decreases to 0 on the order of $1/B$ when B is sufficiently large. On the other hand, if B is 0, obviously the network delay is infinite and no request can be even sent to the cloud, thus $\mathscr{R}(\theta) = 0$. Now if we start to increase B, the network delay becomes from infinite to finite, some requests can have a chance to be processed on time; thus, $\mathscr{R}(\theta)$ will also increase. This predicts that there should exist a cutoff point B^* on network bandwidth B as shown in Fig. 4.5 such that $\mathscr{R}(\theta)$ is increasing and decreasing when $B < B^*$ and $B > B^*$, respectively.

In the following, we use extensive experiments to find such a cutoff point on the network bandwidth and to further obtain insights into the cutoff point.

4.4   Experimental Evaluation

In this section, we set up a small-scale cloud to perform comprehensive experiments to illustrate the resilience factor in a more practical scenario as well as to find the cutoff point on the network bandwidth.

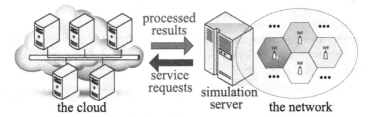

Fig. 4.6 A small-scale cloud is connected to a network simulation server

4.4.1 System Setups

4.4.1.1 Cloud and Network Setups

We set up a small-scale cloud that consists of up to eight computers with Intel CPU i5 2.67 GHz and runs over the Storm framework 0.7.4 [24]. As shown in Fig. 4.6, the cloud is connected to a simulation server that simulates a cellular network environment with mobile nodes moving around according to real-world mobility traces.

In the cellular network, base stations are cloud nodes, and mobile nodes move around, sending service requests to their nearest base stations. These service requests are delivered from the simulation server to the cloud for real-time processing. Then, the processed results in the cloud are sent back to mobile nodes in the simulation environment. The transmission range of mobile nodes and base stations is 750 m, and the cellular network uses TDMA to coordinate all mobile nodes to access the network. The network bandwidth is set to vary from 20 Kbps to 2 Mbps, which is typical for today's cellular networks. The cloud load limit L_{max} is set to be 50. To accommodate node mobility, we choose two sets of mobility traces for mobile nodes from [23].

- NCSU: 35 participants in NC State University campus.
- NewYork: 39 participants in New York City.

4.4.1.2 Mobile Cloud Service

Mobile nodes are set to use a location-aware service $\S(l_s, l_r, f, \sigma)$ supported by the cloud [1, 18]: they periodically send their locations and mobile sensing information via base stations to the cloud, then obtain processed results from the cloud. In particular, the size of service requests l_s is 800 bytes, the size of processed results l_r is 400 bytes, the service frequency f is 0.2 Hz, and the delay requirement for each request σ is 2 s.

4.4.1.3 Performance Measurement

We set quality-of-service requirement $\theta = 95\%$. Then, the resilience factor $R = \mathscr{R}(95\%)$ denotes the maximally allowable percentage of malware-infected nodes in the network such that at least 95 % service requests from legitimate nodes can still be delivered and processed within the 2-s deadline. To measure $\mathscr{R}(95\%)$, we randomly choose malware-infected nodes according to malware infection ratio ρ starting from 0. For a value of ρ, we measure the probability that a request can be processed on time (i.e., $\mathbb{P}(D \leq \sigma)$), and keep increasing ρ until $\rho = \rho^*$ and $\mathbb{P}(D \leq \sigma) < 95\%$. Then, ρ^* equals to the value of the resilience factor, i.e., $\mathscr{R}(95\%)$.

4.4.2 Experimental Results

4.4.2.1 Measuring the Resilience Factor

Our first experiment is to measure the resilience factor under the network-cloud setups to find out the cutoff point predicted in Fig. 4.5. Figure 4.7 shows resilience factor R as a function of network bandwidth B for different numbers of computers M used in the cloud based on NCSU mobility traces. It is observed from Fig. 4.7 that resilience factor R always increases when M increases since more computers used in the cloud means that the cloud is able to process more service requests in a given time period (i.e., the cloud capability C increases). We also see in Fig. 4.7 that as network bandwidth B increases, there indeed exists cutoff points for resilience

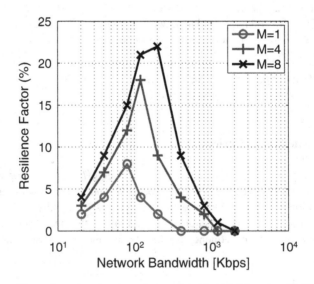

Fig. 4.7 The resilience factor as a function of network bandwidth B based on NCSU traces

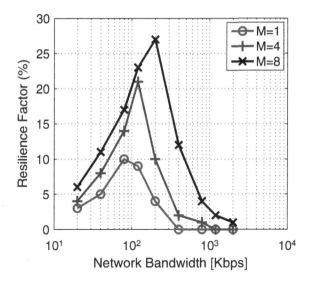

Fig. 4.8 The resilience factor as a function of network bandwidth B based on NewYork traces

factor R: (1) R first increases to the maximum, (2) then R decreases to almost 0, which validates the prediction in Fig. 4.5. In addition, we find that the cutoff point B^* increases when we use more computers to process in the cloud. For example, the cutoff point B^* increases from 80 to 200 Kbps when M goes from 1 to 8. Figure 4.8 shows the malware resilience based on NewYork mobility traces, which demonstrates similar relations between resilience factor R, network bandwidth B, and number of computers M.

Figures 4.7 and 4.8 show that malware resilience of mobile cloud services can be characterized by two distinct regions divided by a cutoff point on the network bandwidth. In the first region, the resilience factor increases as the network bandwidth increases; while in the second region, the resilience factor decreases as the network bandwidth increases.

To further investigate these two distinct regions, we evaluate the performance of the network and cloud individually. In our following experiments, the cloud always consists of eight computers to process service requests (i.e., M is fixed to be 8). We compare the performance between $B = 40$ and $B = 400$ Kbps, because (1) as shown in Figs. 4.7 and 4.8, $B = 40$ Kbps and 400 Kbps are in the regions where resilience factor R increases and decreases, respectively; (2) it can be also seen that these two values of network bandwidth have approximately the same resilience factor for $M = 8$.

With $B = 40$ Kbps and 400 Kbps, we measure the performance of the network and cloud individually. In particular, we use the *network delivery over-due ratio* to denote the probability that the network delivery delay of a service request is larger than the delay requirement of 2 s, and use the *cloud processing over-due ratio* to represent the probability that the cloud processing delay is larger than

Fig. 4.9 The network delivery over-due ratio versus malware infection ratio ρ based on NCSU traces

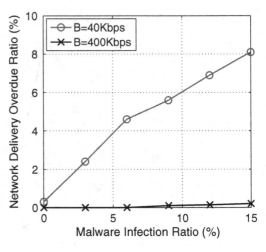

Fig. 4.10 The cloud processing over-due ratio versus malware infection ratio ρ based on NCSU traces

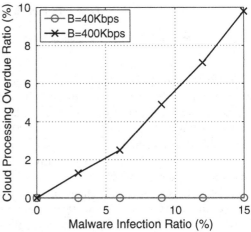

2 s. Figures 4.9 and 4.10 illustrate the network delivery over-due ratio and cloud processing over-due ratio as functions of malware infection ratio ρ based on NCSU traces, respectively. It is noted from Fig. 4.9 that if $B = 40$ Kbps, the network delivery over-due ratio increases significantly as ρ increases (i.e., more nodes are infected by malware). On the other hand, if $B = 400$ Kbps, it is observed that malware almost leads to negligible impacts on the network delivery performance. In contrast, Fig. 4.10 shows exactly the opposite: with ρ increasing, the cloud processing over-due ratio remains zero when $B = 40$ Kbps, but increases significantly when $B = 400$ Kbps.

Remark 4.4. Figures 4.9 and 4.10 show that in malware epidemics, if network bandwidth B is smaller than the cutoff point B^*, the network performance degradation is the dominate factor to worsen the cloud service quality, and the cloud can be very lightly loaded. If $B > B^*$, although the network delivery performance is improved with B increasing, the cloud cannot handle the large amount of service requests from malware-infected nodes, thereby deteriorating the service quality.

Remark 4.5. Our experimental results show that malware resilience of mobile cloud services can be characterized by two distinct regions divided by a cutoff point on the network bandwidth. In the first region, the cloud service quality is limited by the network bandwidth, and thus the resilience factor increases as the network bandwidth increases. We call this region *network-limited region*. In the second region, although the network delivery performance is improved with the network bandwidth increasing, the cloud is not capable of processing large numbers of service requests from malware-infected nodes. As a result, the resilience factor decreases as the network bandwidth increases. We call this region *cloud-limited region* in that malware resilience is fundamentally limited by the cloud capability in this region.

4.4.2.2 Measuring Local Resilience Factors

In previous experiments, we measure the resilience factors over the entire network. We are also interested in local effects on malware resilience; i.e., how resilient the mobile cloud service is on particular areas. To this end, we choose to measure local resilience factors for different zones in the network. For NCSU and New York traces, we randomly select three and two zones for measurement shown in Figs. 4.11 and 4.12, respectively.

Figure 4.13 shows the local resilience factors for $B = 40\,$Kbps (network-limited region) and $B = 400\,$Kbps (cloud-limited region) based on NCSU mobility traces.

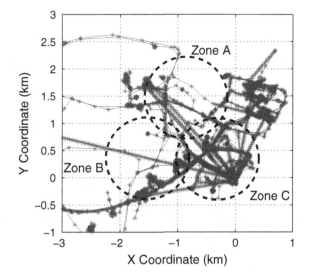

Fig. 4.11 Zones A, B, and C for measuring local resilience factors in NCSU mobility traces

Fig. 4.12 Zones A and B for measuring local resilience factors in NewYork mobility traces

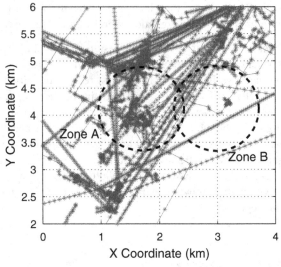

Fig. 4.13 Local resilience factors for zones A, B, and C in NCSU mobility traces

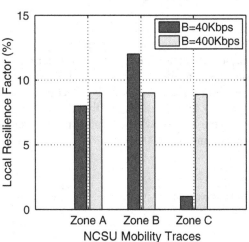

We can see from Fig. 4.13 that when $B = 40$ Kbps, zone C has a much lower resilience factor than zones A and B. It is noted from Fig. 4.11 that zone C is a mobility hotspot. Therefore, on average, there are much more nodes competing the wireless channel in zone C. However, when $B = 400$ Kbps, all the three zones have approximately the same resilience factor. Figure 4.14 illustrates the local resilience factors based on NewYork mobility traces. We can also observe that when $B = 40$ Kbps, zone A, which is a mobility hotspot as shown in Fig. 4.12, has a much lower resilience factor than zone B; but when $B = 400$ Kbps, the two zones have approximately the same resilience factor.

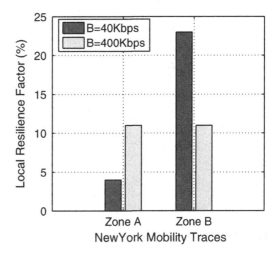

Fig. 4.14 Local resilience factors for zones A and B in NewYork mobility traces

Remark 4.6. Our measurement results with different local areas demonstrate that the network-limited and cloud-limited regions can lead to heterogeneous and homogeneous malware resilience across the network, respectively. In particular, in the network-limited region, local network congestion in mobility hotspots limits the overall resilience factor, and even if the malware infection ratio ρ is larger than the overall resilience factor R in the network (i.e. $\rho > R$), some legitimate nodes may still expect to have the timely cloud service when they are not in mobility hotspots. However, in the cloud-limited region, the cloud service will be globally degraded if $\rho > R$, meaning that all cloud users will experience poor service quality over the entire network.

4.5 Summary and Discussions

In this section, we first summarize our findings then discuss how our results affect the countermeasure design for mobile cloud services against malware attacks.

4.5.1 Summary of Our Results

We have studied the problem of quantifying the malware resilience of mobile cloud services via theoretical analysis and extensive experiments. Our major findings on the resilience factor can be summarized as follows.

- For a practical scenario in which the cloud always has finite capability, there exists a cutoff point B^* on network bandwidth B. If $B < B^*$ (the network-limited

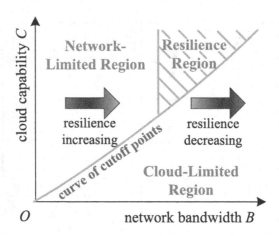

Fig. 4.15 2D malware resilience graph

region), the resilience factor increases with B increasing; If $B > B^*$ (the cloud-limited region), the resilience factor decreases on the order of $1/B$.

- If we increase cloud capability C, the cutoff point B^* will become larger, as shown in Figs. 4.7 and 4.8.
- Strong malware resilience is possible if we keep increasing network bandwidth B and let cloud capability C be on the higher order of B (as indicated in Theorem 4.1).

Combining the findings above, we are able to draw a 2D resilience graph based on network-cloud setups (B, C) in Fig. 4.15 for mobile cloud services. Figure 4.15 summarizes that (1) for any constant cloud capability C, malware resilience first increases in the network-limited region then decreases in the cloud-limited region; (2) the cutoff point B^* also increases with C increasing; (3) there also exists a *resilience region*, in which the resilience factor is always 100 % for B sufficiently large and C on the higher order of B.

4.5.2 Indications to Countermeasure Design

The findings of network-limited and cloud-limited regions are of importance to efficient defense against malware attacks. In particular, for a mobile cloud service under malware attacks,

- If the service is in the network-limited region, local network congestion (especially at mobility hotspots) is found as the main reason for poor service quality. The cloud is in fact not heavily loaded, and may not even observe large numbers of attacking flows from malware-infected nodes. Therefore, countermeasures should be deployed not in the cloud, but in local networks to effectively defend against malware attacks.

- If the service is in the cloud-limited region, cloud overload is identified as the major performance bottleneck. The cloud has to handle a significant amount of service requests from malware-infected nodes, which in turn offer sufficient statistics for attack detection and mitigation. Hence, countermeasures should be deployed in the cloud to efficiently identify and eliminate attack flows.

It is worth noting that in general, it can be difficult to clearly identify whether a mobile cloud service is in the network-limited or cloud-limited region (or to find the exact value of the cutoff point on the network bandwidth). In addition, one of the most popular paradigms for deployment of mobile cloud computing is to build different service clouds with varying capabilities upon the same mobile network infrastructure (e.g., 3G/4G) [9]. This means that in such a system, some cloud services can fall in the network-limited region, while the others are in the cloud-limited region. Therefore, our results in fact encourage deployment of countermeasures in both the network and the cloud to combat malware attacks that can cause damaging impacts to either the network or the cloud.

4.6 Conclusions

In this chapter, we introduced a new metric, resilience factor, to quantify the resilience of mobile cloud services to malware attacks. We found that a mobile cloud service in general falls into one of two resilience regions: network-limited and cloud-limited regions, in which the resilience factor increases and decreases with the network bandwidth increasing, respectively. Our results presented a different perspective on developing network infrastructures for mobile cloud computing: on one hand, increasing the network bandwidth improves the performance of cloud service delivery to mobile users; on the other hand, it can degrade the malware resilience. In addition, our findings in network-limited and cloud-limited regions encourage deployment of countermeasures in both the network and the cloud to efficiently defend against malware attacks.

References

1. Angin P, Bhargava BK (2011) Real-time mobile-cloud computing for context-aware blind navigation. Int J Next Gener Comput 2:1–13
2. Bahl P, Han RY, Li LE, Satyanarayanan M (2012) Advancing the state of mobile cloud computing. In: Proceedings of ACM workshop on mobile cloud computing & services
3. Bhadauria R, Sanyal S (2012) Survey on security issues in cloud computing and associated mitigation techniques. Int J Comput Appl 47:47–66
4. Bianchi G (2000) Performance analysis of the IEEE 802.11 distributed coordination function. IEEE J Sel Areas Commun 18(3):535–547
5. Chun BG, Maniatis P (2010) Dynamically partitioning applications between weak devices and clouds. In: Proceedings of ACM workshop on mobile cloud computing & services

6. Constantinescu L, Kim J, Feng D (2012) SparkMed: a framework for dynamic integration of multimedia medical data into distributed m-health systems. IEEE Trans Inf Technol Biomed 16(1):40–52
7. Cox PA (2011) Build a more secure, mobile cloud environment – common mobile cloud vulnerabilities and solutions to secure them. developerWorks
8. Cuervo E, Balasubramanian A, ki Cho D (2010) MAUI: making smartphones last longer with code offload. In: Proceedings of ACM Mobisys 2010
9. Dinh HT, Lee C, Niyato D, Wang P (2011) A survey of mobile cloud computing: architecture, applications, and approaches. Wirel Commun Mob Comput 13:1587–1611
10. Felt AP, Finifter M, Chin E, Hanna S, Wagner D (2011) A survey of mobile malware in the wild. In: Proceedings of ACM workshop on security and privacy in smartphones and mobile devices
11. Hadoop (2015). http://hadoop.apache.org/
12. Iosup A, Yigitbasi N, Epema D (2011) On the performance variability of production cloud services. In: Proceedings of IEEE/ACM international symposium on cluster, cloud and grid computing
13. Jung E, Wang Y, Prilepov I, Maker F, Liu X, Akella V (2010) User-profile-driven collaborative bandwidth sharing on mobile phones. In: Proceedings of ACM workshop on mobile cloud computing & services
14. Juniper Networks (2011) Malicious mobile threats report 2010/2011
15. Kavulya S, Tan J, Gandhi R, Narasimhan P (2010) An analysis of traces from a production MapReduce cluster. In: Proceedings of IEEE/ACM international conference on cluster, cloud and grid computing
16. Khouzani MR, Sarkar S, Altman E (2011) A dynamic game solution to malware attack. In: Proceedings of IEEE INFOCOM '11
17. Kounelis I, Lochner J, Shaw D, Scheer S (2012) Security of service requests for cloud based m-commerce. In: Proceedings of international convention MIPRO '12
18. Kumar K, Lu YH (2010) Cloud computing for mobile users: can offloading computation save energy? Computer 43:51–56
19. Lookout Mobile Security (2011) Mobile threat report
20. McAfee Labs (2011) McAfee threats report: third quarter 2011
21. Mulliner C, Seifert JP (2010) Rise of the iBots: owning a telco network. In: Proceedings of international conference on malicious and unwanted software
22. Ra M, Sheth A, Mummert L, Pillai P, Wetherall D, Govindan R (2011) Odessa: enabling interactive perception applications on mobile devices. In: Proceedings of ACM Mobisys 2011
23. Rhee I, Shin M, Hong S, Lee K, Kim S, Chong S (2009) CRAWDAD data set ncsu/mobilitymodels (v. 2009-07-23)
24. Storm (2015). http://storm-project.net/
25. Tan J, Meng X, Zhang L (2012) Performance analysis of coupling scheduler for MapReduce/Hadoop. In: Proceedings of IEEE INFOCOM '12
26. Traynor P, Lin M, Ongtang M, Rao V, Jaeger T, McDaniel P, Porta TL (2009) On cellular botnets: measuring the impact of malicious devices on a cellular network core. In: Proceedings of ACM conference on computer and communications security (CCS)
27. Xiao Y, Hui P, Savolainen P (2011) CasCap: cloud-assisted context-aware power management for mobile devices. In: Proceedings of the second international workshop on mobile cloud computing and services
28. Zohar E, Cidon I, Mokryn O (2011) The power of prediction: cloud bandwidth and cost reduction. In: Proceedings of ACM SIGCOMM '11

Printed in the United States
By Bookmasters